Ju PROF B Rou
Pascal
Arthur
22.00

W9-AIV-893

PRINCETON PUBLIC LIBRARY

3 1945 00308 8704

WITHDRAWN

**Purchased by the
Princeton Public Library
Princeton, New Jersey,
with funds donated by the
Friends of the Library**

Arthur Conan Doyle

Beyond Baker Street

OXFORD
PORTRAITS

Arthur Conan Doyle

Beyond Baker Street

Janet B. Pascal

Oxford University Press

New York • Oxford

PUBLIC LIBRARY, PRINCETON, NJ

For my mother and father

OXFORD
UNIVERSITY PRESS

Oxford   New York
Athens   Auckland   Bangkok   Bogotá   Buenos Aires   Calcutta
Cape Town   Chennai   Dar es Salaam   Delhi   Florence   Hong Kong   Istanbul
Karachi   Kuala Lumpur   Madrid   Melbourne   Mexico City   Mumbai
Nairobi   Paris   São Paulo   Singapore   Taipei   Tokyo   Toronto   Warsaw
and associated companies in
Berlin   Ibadan

Copyright © 2000 by Janet B. Pascal
Published by Oxford University Press, Inc.
198 Madison Avenue, New York, New York 10016
Web site: www.oup.com

Oxford is a registered trademark of Oxford University Press

All rights reserved. No part of this publication
may be reproduced, stored in a retrieval system, or transmitted,
in any form or by any means, electronic, mechanical,
photocopying, recording, or otherwise, without the prior
permission of Oxford University Press.

Design and layout: Greg Wozney
Picture research: Patricia Burns

Library of Congress Cataloging-in-Publication Data
Pascal, Janet B.
Arthur Conan Doyle: beyond Baker Street / by Janet B, Pascal.
p. cm. — (Oxford portraits series)
Includes bibliographical references and index.
ISBN 0-19-512262-3 (alk. paper)
1. Doyle, Arthur Conan, Sir, 1859–1930. 2. Detective and mystery
stories—Authorship. 3. Authors, Scottish—19th century—Biography.
4. Holmes, Sherlock (Fictitious character) 5. Spiritualists—Great
Britain—Biography. 6.Physicians—Great Britain—Biography.
I. Title. II. Series.
PR4623.P34   1999
823' .8—dc21   99-36643
[B]   CIP

9 8 7 6 5 4 3 2 1

Printed in the United States of America
on acid-free paper

On the cover: A formal portrait of Arthur Conan Doyle from the time of the Boer
War in Africa.

Frontispiece: Arthur Conan Doyle, motor fanatic, on his motorbike at Undershaw
in 1905.

CONTENTS

This cartoon shows Conan Doyle chained to Sherlock Holmes. Conan Doyle sometimes felt that he would never be able to escape from his most famous creation.

PREFACE

What is your favorite Sherlock Holmes story? Under the circumstances, this seems an odd question for a reporter to ask. Amid the chaos of a South African military hospital, the man from the *Illustrated London News* had seized a moment to interview the hospital's supervising doctor. In 1900, the Boer War was at its height, the hospital was overwhelmed with a typhoid fever epidemic, and dead and dying men crowded the floor between the overflowing cots. The supervisor, desperately busy, could not help being irritated when the reporter spouted such a frivolous question. But, as always, he tried to be courteous. "Perhaps the one about the serpent," he replied. "But for the life of me I can't remember the name of it."

With his energy concentrated on saving men's lives, it is not surprising that a doctor would not want to waste his time on popular detective fiction. But even so, he might have been expected to remember at least the title of the story. (It's "The Adventure of the Speckled Band.") After all, he was Arthur Conan Doyle, and he had written it himself.

The pattern of Conan Doyle's entire life can be seen in this brief exchange. Wherever there was excitement or danger, wherever important events were taking place, wherever he felt he could be useful, Arthur Conan Doyle could be found near the front lines, enthusiastically doing twice as much work as anyone else, having a wonderful time, and helping to lift everyone else's spirits. Nevertheless, whether he was harpooning whales in the Arctic, competing with German officers in a road race, introducing skis to the Alps, or fighting to save a wrongly condemned man from the gallows, in the eyes of the public, he was always the creator of Sherlock Holmes, and the public never let him forget it. Even at his own wedding, he could not escape his fictional creation. The next day a newspaper in Buenos Aires announced SHERLOCK HOLMES QUIETLY MARRIED. It is no wonder that he often longed to kill off the famous detective.

Today most people know Arthur Conan Doyle only as the man who created Sherlock Holmes. The Holmes stories were a tiny part of his literary output and something he never took very seriously, but they are enough to ensure his lasting fame when his more serious works are almost forgotten. Sherlock Holmes is one of the most familiar figures in modern culture, readily recognized not only in English-speaking countries but around the world. His existence is believed in by more people than any other fictional character's. Over a century after he first appeared in 1887, he still receives almost 200 letters a month at his legendary address of 221B Baker Street. He has appeared in advertisements, picture books, and even on the science fiction television series *Star Trek*. People who have never read a Sherlock Holmes story immediately know that a character who wears an Inverness cape and a deerstalker cap and smokes a curved pipe—Holmes's popular image—must be a detective.

In his own day, although Sherlock Holmes always attracted more than his fair share of attention, Conan Doyle was renowned for many other reasons. He wrote several popular best-selling books, including *The White Company,* a novel of chivalry set in 1366 and considered at the time one of the greatest historical novels ever written, and *The Lost World,* in which, long before the book and movie *Jurassic Park,* he imagined a land where dinosaurs still lived. He wrote meticulous and accurate histories of the great wars he experienced, and exerted a tremendous influence on public opinion with his political writings. He was among the first to realize the changes submarines and armored tanks would bring to modern warfare and to try to prepare Great Britain for what it would face in World War I. And for the last quarter of his life, he was a fervent spiritualist who abandoned everything else to devote himself to speaking with the dead at seances and spreading the spiritualist message throughout the world. Arthur Conan Doyle hoped to be remembered as a prophet of spiritualism, but instead his name will be linked forever to the most famously literal-minded character in literature, Sherlock Holmes, who would never believe in ghosts.

Six-year-old Arthur Conan Doyle with his father, Charles. Arthur is wearing the velvet and lace suit made popular by the book Little Lord Fauntleroy.

THE STUDENT ON HIS NARROW BED

Arthur Conan Doyle was born into an ancient and aristo-cratic Irish Catholic family. The Doyles could trace their lineage all the way back to the 12th-century French noble family of D'oel or D'Ouilly, while his mother's family had connections with the Conans and the royal Percy and Plantagenet families of England. From the time he was a small child, this heritage captured Arthur's imagination. His mother was obsessed with the family's past. One of Arthur's earliest memories was of sitting on the kitchen table learn-ing from her the coats of arms of all his noble ancestors. She filled her small son's mind with tales of chivalry, and he grew up dreaming of knights, sacrifice, and battle, and being aware that he must always follow the code of a chival-rous knight: fight for what is right and defend the weak.

When he wrote his autobiography, *Memories and Adventures,* although he was obviously anxious not to appear vain, he could not resist beginning with an outline of his illustrious ancestry. "One has, therefore," he remarked diffi-dently, "some strange strains in one's blood which are noble in origin and, one can but hope, are noble in tendency." As an adult he used his middle and last names, Conan and

A bookplate bearing Arthur Conan Doyle's coat of arms. As a small boy, Conan Doyle learned the rules of heraldry from his mother, who was very proud of her noble ancestry. The motto means "By strength he conquers."

Doyle, together to display both sides of his heritage.

On his father's side, some distinguished ancestors were still living. His grandfather, John Doyle, was the most famous satirical artist of his day. John Doyle's three oldest sons were also very successful artists, especially Richard or "Dicky" Doyle, who, as an illustrator at *Punch* magazine, was known to all of Victorian society. The youngest son, Charles, who would become Arthur's father, was the unsuccessful Doyle. When he was 19 years old he was sent away to Edinburgh to take a job as an architect in the Government Office of Works. Although his family was careful to place him in a boardinghouse run by a respectable Catholic family, he was lonely and unhappy in the strange city. He remained there all his life, in the same job, making no mark on the world. He earned a little extra money from his paintings and illustrations, but he did not have the artistic success of others in his family. He married Mary Foley, the daughter of his landlady.

Arthur was born to Charles and Mary in Edinburgh on May 22, 1859, the second child—after his sister Annette— and the first son. Two more sisters followed soon after. He was his mother's favorite, and remained extremely close to her until she died. His was a troubled household. Charles Doyle felt thwarted and confined by life. He painted powerful, disturbing paintings that he could not sell. As an adult, Arthur Conan Doyle remembered him as a "great and original artist—far the greatest . . . in the family," but his talent was never recognized. Although he worked hard at a job that held no interest for him, his income was barely enough to support the members of his family in the style of living he considered appropriate to people of their class. They were not poverty-stricken, but they were always on the edge. Visits from his more successful brothers were embarrassing. Mary struggled to run the household and eventually had to take in a boarder for extra income. In his unhappiness, Charles looked for escape by drinking, and became an alcoholic.

Arthur went to the local school run by a "pock-marked, one-eyed rascal who might have stepped from the pages of Dickens." He spent much of his spare time reading, and checked out so many books that, he claimed in *Memories and Adventures,* "It is rumoured that a special meeting of a library committee was held in my honour, at which a bye-law was passed that no subscriber should be permitted to change his book more than three times a day." He enjoyed the rough life of the streets, and got into a lot of fights, which he usually won. His mother wanted to save her precious son from the bad influences of this atmosphere. Despite their precarious financial state, she was determined to send him to a good school. His father insisted it must be a Catholic school, so when he was ten, he left for Stonyhurst, a well-known English boarding school run by Jesuits. They offered to take Arthur for nothing if he would promise to dedicate his life to the Catholic Church as a priest, but his mother foresaw a greater future for him. Somehow, the money was raised to pay his fees.

In later life, Arthur did not have fond memories of Stonyhurst. For the first two years—spent in Hodder, a separate preparatory school, with the younger boys—although Arthur was homesick, he was not too unhappy. When he moved up to the main school, life became more harsh. Stonyhurst was run on medieval principles. The curriculum devoted one year to each of the seven standard medieval subjects: elements, figures, rudiments, grammar, syntax, poetry, and rhetoric, obsolete terms that in practice meant Euclidean geometry, algebra, and the Greek and Latin classics, taught by rote. Even Arthur, who was already writing verses and reading poetry and French novels for fun, found the lessons dull. This system could only be excused, he later said, "on the plea that any exercise, however stupid in itself, forms a sort of mental dumbbell by which one can improve one's mind."

Except for one six-week vacation in the summer, the students spent the entire year at school. They slept in cold, bare dormitories, getting up at 5:30 in the morning to wash in cold water and eat a breakfast of dry bread and hot, watered milk. Other meals were almost as Spartan, often consisting of dry bread, fish, potatoes, and, as Conan Doyle described it in his autobiography, "a most extraordinary drink, which was brown but had no other characteristic of beer." The boys were never left alone; a priest watched them at all times, day and night, which at least prevented the bullying that was common in most English boarding schools, but created an oppressive lack of privacy.

Arthur was rebellious under all this supervision and got into as much mischief as he could. He fought the other boys, smoked, and sneaked away when possible to buy forbidden food and wink at the town girls. Stonyhurst believed in punishment. The most common penalty was nine blows on each hand with a piece of India-rubber called a tolley. This punishment was severe enough to make the hands turn black and blue and swell up so that the boy could not turn a door handle or hold a pen. "I think few, if any, boys of my time endured more of it," Arthur claimed, rather proudly. The worst offenders were beaten with a birch rod.

At school Arthur began to write the frequent letters to his mother that he continued all her life. He called her "the Ma'am." This poem he sent her during his first year away sums up his opinion of Stonyhurst:

> The student he lay on his narrow bed
> He dreamt not of the morrow. . . .
> He thought of the birch's stinging stroke
> And he thought with fear of the morrow
> He wriggled and tumbled and nearly awoke
> And again he sighed with sorrow.

School holidays provided a break from Stonyhurst's regular strict regime. One of these was Father Rector's Day, in which, in odd contrast to their usual austerity, the masters supplied the boys with cigars, and they all went out skating in the moonlight while the masters threw firecrackers at them. During the Christmas holidays, too, although the boys had to stay at the school, life was very different. Arthur wrote to his mother that during one Christmas revel, he and three friends ate "two turkeys, one very large goose, two chickens, one large ham and two pieces of ham, two large sausages, seven boxes of sardines, one of lobster, a plate full of tarts, and seven pots of jam. In the way of drink we had five bottles of sherry, five of port, one of claret and two of raspberry vinegar; we had also two bottles of pickles."

School life also offered some more frequent compensations—especially sports. Arthur was a big boy, tall, strong, and broad-shouldered. He excelled in cricket (a game resembling baseball), hockey, rugby, fishing, billiards, and swimming, and particularly loved boxing. He led the cricket team every year, and the other boys looked up to him. "When I reside at Edinburgh, I would like to enter some cricket club there. It is a jolly game, and does more to make a fellow strong and healthy than all the doctors in the world," he wrote to his mother. He retained his enthusiasm for sports, and the confidence that they gave him, all his life.

Arthur's love for literature blossomed, although not from anything he was taught in class. Every spare minute he spent reading (even managing to evade the priests and read under the covers at night). He enjoyed the adventure stories of Mayne Reid and the historic romances of Sir Walter Scott, but his greatest enthusiasm was for Thomas Babington Macaulay, the poet and historian, who restored to Arthur the love for history that his boring school lessons had deadened. While working on the "dreary unnatural task" of churning out verse on subjects set by the teachers, he found that he not only enjoyed writing but was very good at it. By his final year he was editor of the school magazine.

His first story, written at five years old, had been a thriller about a man-eating tiger. Now he turned this talent for exciting fiction to good use, making up action-packed stories for his schoolmates—and charging jam tarts for them. He would stop at the most suspenseful moment in the story and refuse to continue until he was supplied with another tart. "I always stipulated for tarts 'down' and strict business," he recalled.

Arthur stayed at Stonyhurst for six years. He later claimed that he was an indifferent student and the masters had a low opinion of him, recalling that when he was leav-

A group of cricket players at Stonyhurst, where Arthur attended school for six years. He is the tall boy on the right holding the cricket ball.

ing the school, one of them said to him, "Doyle, I have known you now for seven years, and I know you thoroughly. I am going to say something which you will remember in after-life. Doyle, you will never come to any good." However, their letters to his parents show that most of the masters actually thought quite highly of him, and when he took the matriculation exams given to boys who had completed the school course, he passed with honors. This meant that he was eligible to go on to a university, but his parents and teachers felt that at 16 he was still a little young. So the Jesuit fathers suggested that he should attend Feldkirch, the Jesuit school in Vorarlberg, Austria, for a year.

Arthur found this an easy and pleasant year after the rigors of Stonyhurst. The dormitories were heated and food was plentiful. He did not learn much German, because he stuck with the other English boys, but what he did learn would be useful to him later in life. Continuing his omnivorous reading, he discovered Edgar Allan Poe, whose detective stories "The Gold Bug" and "The Murders in the Rue Morgue" would have a great influence on him. There were no games of cricket, but the boys went hiking in the mountains and played a strange game like soccer, only on stilts.

Perhaps most fun of all, he was drafted into the school band. Because he was so large and strong, Arthur was chosen to play the huge brass horn called a bombardon, on which he performed in "a measured rhythm with an occasional run, which sounds like a hippopotamus doing a stepdance." The big, showy, dramatic instrument, resembling a tuba, suited his extroverted personality perfectly. He wrote to his mother,

> The soundest sleeper, far or near
> I think would scarcely slumber on,
> If close to his unconscious ear
> You played upon the Bombardon.

In addition to writing doggerel verse, he founded a student paper, the *Feldkirch Gazette*. He took as its motto "Fear not, and put it in print," a saying that he followed his whole life. Unfortunately, he put the motto in practice by writing an editorial criticizing the Jesuit teachers' custom of censoring the boys' letters, and they shut the paper down. Arthur's uncle, the distinguished journalist Michael Conan, thought the paper showed talent, and suggested that Arthur should become a writer, but Arthur did not take this idea seriously. He needed to do something that would earn money to help support his family, which by now included three sisters, Annette, Lottie, and Connie, and a brother, Innes.

And so, after this restful interlude, Arthur found himself back in Edinburgh, trying to face up to the question of what to do with his life. He had enjoyed himself, but felt he had "little to show, either mental or spiritual, for my pleasant school year" in Feldkirch. It had been decided that he would become a doctor—not because he had any particular interest, but because it was a respectable profession that paid well, and because since Edinburgh University was home to one of the finest medical schools, he could save money by living at home. Arthur had no real enthusiasm for the idea of being a doctor, but he went along with it. "The situation called for energy and application so that one was bound to try to meet it," he remembered in *Memories and Adventures,* turning medical school into a kind of chivalric challenge. "My mother had been so splendid that we could not fail her."

Because money was so scarce, Arthur decided that he was going to win a scholarship, and as usual when he set out to do something, he succeeded. When he went to collect the money, however, he discovered that through a clerical error it had already been given away—to someone else. And so he had to be content with honor and no money.

"One Long Weary Grind"

This unfair loss of his scholarship set the tone for Conan Doyle's entire medical school experience, which he described in *Memories and Adventures* as "one long weary grind at botany, chemistry, anatomy, physiology, and a whole list of compulsory subjects, many of which have a very indirect bearing upon the art of curing." Outside of school, he continued to enjoy life, being gifted with, in his words, "an eager nature which missed nothing in the way of fun which could be gathered, and . . . a great capacity for enjoyment." He continued to read heavily. Out of his tight budget, he had allotted threepence per day for lunch. On his way to class, he passed a used bookstore with a shelf of books for threepence, and often he added to his book collection and skipped lunch. He played sports, went to the theater and to dances, and flirted with as many girls as he could. On one occasion, while waiting in line outside a theater, he got into a fight with six soldiers at once, defending the honor of a lady who had been pinched.

To amuse himself, he started writing short stories in the hope of earning a little extra money. To his delight, one of the first stories he sent out was accepted. "The Mystery of

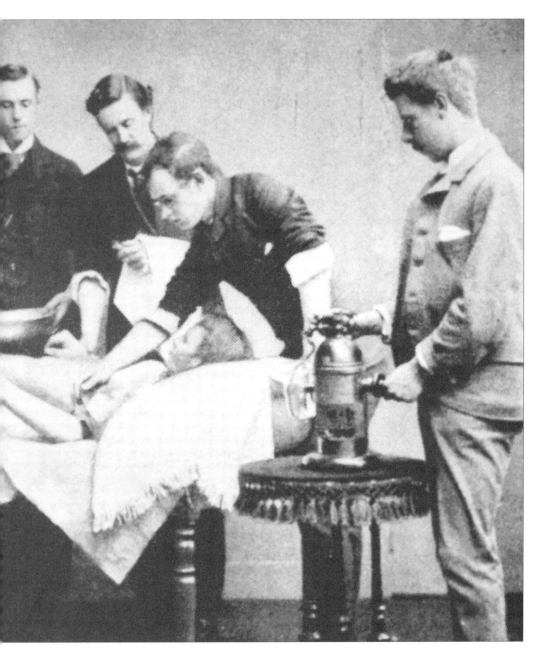

A surgical operation from the time when Conan Doyle was a medical student at Edinburgh. The canister on the right holds carbolic spray, the first antiseptic, which was pioneered by Joseph Lister in 1865 only 14 years before Conan Doyle began his studies. It helped bring medicine into the modern age.

Sasassa Valley" appeared anonymously in *Chambers's Journal* in October 1879. It was based on a South African legend about a demon with glowing eyes that, when the heroes investigate, turn out to be diamonds. This crude short story already contained many elements that would become familiar in his later writing. It is a mystery, full of excitement and adventure, with a hint of the strange and otherworldly and a logical solution. The good luck of getting one of his very first efforts published gave him confidence, and another story appeared before he graduated. These stories were published anonymously, as was the custom in magazines at the time.

Conan Doyle also continued writing comic verse for his own amusement. This ditty was scrawled in the margin of one of his textbooks:

I'll tell you a most serious fact,
That opium dries a mucous tract,
And constipates and causes thirst,
And stimulates the heart at first,
And then allows its strength to fall,
Relaxing the capillary wall.
The cerebrum is first affected,
On tetanus you mustn't bet,
Secretions gone except the sweat.
Lungs and sexuals don't forget.

The boring routine of medical school was enlivened by some unusual personalities among the professors. He was "fascinated and awed" by Professor William Rutherford, a loud, forceful, and boisterously confident man who began his lectures in a booming voice from the hall before he entered the classroom. Conan Doyle later used Rutherford as the model for Professor Challenger in his popular science fiction series.

The professor who would have the most profound influence on his later life, however, was the distinguished surgeon Joseph Bell. Bell took an interest in Conan Doyle

Licensed to kill

This sketch, which
Conan Doyle drew of
himself when he
received his degree,
reflects the humorously
self-deprecating tone
he used when speaking
of his medical skill.
He said that in
medical school he was
"always one of the
ruck—a 60% man at
examinations"—a
claim that is not borne
out by his teachers'
comments.

("for some reason I have never understood," Conan Doyle says modestly in *Memories and Adventures*) and hired him as his out-patient clerk. Conan Doyle's job was to meet patients in the outer room, find out the basic facts of their illness, and then bring them into the clinic, where Bell "sat in state surrounded by his dressers [assistants] and students." Bell would then diagnose and treat them in front of the crowd. He was renowned among the students for his uncanny ability to deduce personal facts about the patients just by looking at them, before they opened their mouths.

Conan Doyle later borrowed the theatrical fashion in which Bell showed off his deductive talents for Sherlock Holmes. Many students have written recollections of Bell's performances. This scene, a reminiscence published in 1956 in the *Lancet,* a prominent medical journal, is typical. (The participants are represented as speaking in Scots dialect.)

A woman with a small child was shown in. Joe Bell said good morning to her and she said good morning in reply.

"What sort of crossing did ye have fra' Burntisland?"

"It was guid."

"And had ye a guid walk up Inverleith Row?"

"Yes."

"And what did ye do with th'other wain?"

"I left him with my sister in Leith."

"And would ye still be working at the linoleum factory?"

"Yes I am."

"You see gentlemen, when she said good morning to me I noticed her Fife accent, and, as you know, the nearest town in Fife is Burntisland. You noticed the red clay on the edges of the soles of her shoes, and the only such clay within twenty miles of Edinburgh is in the Botanical Gardens. Inverleith Row borders the gardens and is her nearest way here from Leith. You observed that the coat she carried over her arm is too big for the child who is with her, and therefore she set out from home with two children. Finally she has a dermatitis on the fingers of the right hand which is peculiar to workers in the linoleum factory at Burntisland."

Of course Bell sometimes made mistakes. Once he deduced—correctly—that a patient played in a band, explaining to the gathered students that he had realized this because the man's cheek muscles were paralyzed by blowing too hard on wind instruments. He then asked the patient what instrument he played and was told, "The big drum." Still, as Conan Doyle said, "It is no wonder that after the study of such a character I used and amplified his methods when in later life I tried to build up a scientific detective who solved cases on his own merits and not through the folly of the criminal."

Although Conan Doyle later claimed he was only a mediocre medical student, Bell remembered, "I always regarded him as one of the best students I ever had. He was exceedingly interested always upon anything connected with diagnosis, and was never tired of trying to discover those little details which one looks for."

Conan Doyle was eager to ease the financial burden on his family as soon as possible. He squeezed a year's course work into half a year, so that he could use the other half to earn money. By his third year he felt ready to offer himself as a medical assistant to do odd jobs and help make up medicines. His first employer, a Dr. Richardson, worked among the poor people of Sheffield. Conan Doyle lasted only three weeks. "These Sheffielders would rather be poisoned by a man with a beard than be saved by a man without one," he complained. Later, looking back, he admitted that, although "I had horse sense enough to save myself and my employer from any absolute catastrophe," he was so inexperienced that his assistance was not worth much. He once sent out pill boxes carefully wrapped, with elaborate instructions, but forgot to put the pills inside.

Dr. Joseph Bell believed that "the precise and intelligent recognition and appreciation of minor differences is the real essential factor in all successful medical diagnosis." This way of thinking became the basis for Sherlock Holmes's methods of detection.

Then he received an offer to join a Dr. Elliot in his quiet country practice at a tiny village oddly named Ruyton-of-the-Eleven-Towns. Here he faced his first medical emergency. An old cannon had exploded at a party, injuring one of the bystanders, and Elliot was away. "On arriving there I found a man in bed with a lump of iron sticking out of the side of his head. I tried not to show the alarm which I felt, and I did the obvious thing by pulling out the iron." Finding that the skull was not broken, he stitched up the wound, and was confident from then on that he would be able to perform his duties as a doctor.

For these first jobs he had received only room and board, but once he had some experience, he felt he could request an actual salary. The next summer he worked for Dr. Reginald Ratcliff Hoare in the city of Birmingham, seeing some patients on his own. He became good friends with the Hoare family and returned to work with the doctor again the next year. While with Hoare, he published his first piece of medical research—an article called "Gelseminum as a Poison." With the same dedication to scientific research that Sherlock Holmes would later exhibit, he conducted research on himself, taking gradually increasing amounts of gelseminum so he could see when it began to have an ill effect. He did not stop until the dizziness, headaches, blurred vision, depression, diarrhea, and sleeplessness began to affect his ability to work.

It was as well that Conan Doyle was earning money now, because the financial situation at home had become desperate. Two more sisters, Ida and Julia, had been born, for a total of five girls. His father's health had broken down and, at only the age of 47, he had to leave his job and move into a convalescent home. Charles Doyle spent the rest of his life in institutions, suffering from epilepsy, depression, and alcoholism, and sometimes considered insane. Arthur's sister Annette, and later two other sisters, went abroad to become governesses, and the money they could send back home was practically the family's only income.

During Conan Doyle's third year of medical school, a fellow student made him an exciting proposition. He had a job offer which he was unable to take and wondered if Conan Doyle would be interested. "Would you care," he asked, "to start next week for a whaling cruise? You'll be surgeon, two pound ten a month and three shillings a ton oil money." (This was about $11 a month plus a share of the profits, at a time when $1,500 could support a family for a year.) This was exactly the kind of challenge Arthur Conan Doyle loved. He set sail on the *Hope* on February 28, 1880. For the rest of his life he would remember the Arctic voyage as one of the high points of his life.

FROM *A STUDY IN SCARLET*

Sherlock Holmes often shows his uncanny talents by correctly characterizing a complete stranger. Conan Doyle closely modeled these scenes on the displays of reasoning given by Dr. Joseph Bell. Since Holmes is a fictional character, with the author on his side, his conclusions are always right. In real life, of course, the details he notes would be open to other interpretations. In the early days, Watson is skeptical, as this exchange from A Study in Scarlet *demonstrates.*

"I wonder what that fellow is looking for?" I asked, pointing to a stalwart, plainly dressed individual who was walking slowly down the other side of the street, looking anxiously at the numbers. He had a large blue envelope in his hand, and was evidently the bearer of a message.

"You mean the retired sergeant of Marines," said Sherlock Holmes.

"Brag and bounce!" thought I to myself. "He knows that I cannot verify his guess."

The thought had hardly passed through my mind when the man whom we were watching caught sight of the number on our door, and ran rapidly across the roadway. We heard a loud knock, a deep voice below, and heavy steps ascending the stair.

"For Mr. Sherlock Holmes," he said, stepping into the room and handing my friend the letter.

Here was an opportunity of taking the conceit out of him. He little thought of this when he made that random shot. "May I ask, my lad," I said, in the blandest voice, "what your trade may be?"

"Commissionaire, sir," he said, gruffly. "Uniform away for repairs."

"And you were?" I asked, with a slightly malicious glance at my companion.

"A sergeant, sir, Royal Marine Light Infantry, sir. No answer? Right, sir." He clicked his heels together, raised his hand in a salute, and was gone.

I confess that I was considerably startled by this fresh proof of the practical nature of my companion's theories. My respect for his powers of analysis increased wondrously. There still remained some lurking suspicion in my mind, however, that the whole thing was a pre-arranged episode, intended to dazzle me, though what earthly object he could have in taking me in was past my comprehension. When I looked at him he had finished reading the note, and his eyes had assumed the vacant, lack-lustre expression which showed mental abstraction.

"How in the world did you deduce that?" I asked.

"Deduce what?" said he, petulantly.

"Why, that he was a retired sergeant of Marines."

"I have no time for trifles," he answered, brusquely, then with a smile, "Excuse my rudeness. You broke the thread of my thoughts; but perhaps it is as well. So you actually were not able to see that that man was a sergeant of Marines?"

"No, indeed."

"It was easier to know it than to explain why I know it. If you were asked to prove that two and two made four, you might find some difficulty, and yet you are quite sure of the fact. Even across the street I could see a great blue anchor tattooed on the back of the fellow's hand. That smacked of the sea. He had a military carriage, however, and regulation side whiskers. There we have the marine. He was a man with some amount of self-importance and a certain air of command. You must have observed the way in which he held his head and swung his cane. A steady, respectable, middle-aged man, too, on the face of him—all facts which led me to believe that he had been a sergeant."

"Wonderful!" I ejaculated.

"Commonplace," said Holmes.

THE *HOPE* AND THE *MAYUMBA*

As soon as Conan Doyle boarded, the steward of the *Hope* challenged him to a boxing match. This contest provided a welcome chance to prove himself, for Conan Doyle was much more secure in his boxing skills than in his medical knowledge. That night, through the thin walls, he overheard his opponent telling the others, "He's the best surgeon we've had—he's blacked my eye." After this promising start, Conan Doyle found to his relief that his services as a doctor were actually not very likely to be needed.

Conan Doyle became friendly with the captain and crew. The steward he had boxed turned out to have a good tenor voice and often spent the evening singing sentimental songs to the crew. (Later this steward became a baker in the service of Queen Victoria.) He spent one evening pulling two battling officers off each other over and over. The cook got drunk and ruined dinner three days in a row, until one sailor sobered him up for good by hitting him over the head with a frying pan so hard that his head went right through the bottom, and the pan hung around his neck like a collar.

Before going after whales, the ship spent some time

In this photograph taken on board the Hope *in 1880, the 21-year-old Arthur Conan Doyle, ship's surgeon, is third from the left.*

hunting in seal breeding grounds. One morning Conan Doyle awoke to the sound of ice striking the ship, and went up for his first sight of the fields of icebergs, which he never forgot. "I went on deck to see the whole sea covered with them to the horizon. . . . Their dazzling whiteness made the sea seem bluer by contrast, and with a blue sky above, and that glorious Arctic air in one's nostrils, it was a morning to remember."

With his usual eagerness for new experiences, Conan Doyle wanted to join the hunters as they climbed off the ship onto the icebergs. The captain refused to let him, however. The sea was rough, and it would be dangerous for an inexperienced man. Sulkily, Conan Doyle settled down on the side of the ship to watch—but he sat on a sheet of ice and slid right off the ship into the freezing water. He managed to pull himself up onto an iceberg, and the captain told him that he might as well go out with the men, because he seemed determined to fall into the sea anyway. Conan Doyle was delighted, and he justified the captain's faith by falling into the water twice more. "I finished ignominiously by having to take to my bed while all my clothes were drying in the engine-room," he admitted. Conan Doyle was always able to laugh at himself and did not mind the teasing he had to endure from the crew. From then on they called him the "Great Northern Diver."

Although it was not part of his duties as ship's surgeon, he joined the crew in their work, killing and skinning mother and baby seals. It was the first time he had witnessed this kind of slaughter—a "murderous harvest," he called it—and he found it upsetting. "It is brutal work," he wrote. "Those glaring crimson pools upon the dazzling white of the icefields, under the peaceful silence of a blue Arctic sky, did seem a horrible intrusion." But he enjoyed the sport, and justified it to himself by thinking that it was "not more brutal than that which goes on to supply every dinner-table in the country," and that the seals were a useful part of the

economy bringing work to "the long line of seamen, dock-
ers, tanners, curers, triers, chandlers, leather merchants, and
oil-sellers."

When the crew finished with the seals, the ship moved
farther north to the whaling grounds. Conan Doyle took a
place in one of the whaling boats, where he performed so
well that the captain offered to take him on as a whaler. In
Memories and Adventures, he gives an enthusiastically vivid
picture of the violent and brutal process of harpooning a
whale. It was physically demanding and dangerous, and
required teamwork—the kind of experience he would seek
out all his life. He enjoyed himself thoroughly, and he did
not let the brutality bother him because he believed the
whale felt no pain. Describing the death of a whale in a pro-
longed struggle that threatened to swamp the boat, he said,
"Who would swap that moment for any other triumph that
sport can give?" In his later life, Conan Doyle's conscience
led him to give up hunting altogether—but only regretfully,
for he never lost his love for the excitement of the chase.

It is hard to sympathize today with the pleasure he
found in this bloody business, which he treated as a kind of
sport, but he did bring back several things of indisputable
value from the trip. First, of course, there was the money. It
was more than he had ever been able to give his mother
before, and he pleased himself by hiding gold pieces in all
the pockets of her clothing, so that she would have the

The Hope, *the Arctic
whaler on which
Conan Doyle got his
first taste of the adven-
turous outdoor life he
loved. "I came of age
in 80 degrees north
latitude," he claimed.*

33

excitement of finding them. He thought that he had never been so healthy before, and believed the trip had a permanent effect on his health. "I have no doubt," he wrote, "that my physical health during my whole life has been affected by that splendid air, and that the inexhaustible store of energy which I have enjoyed is to some extent drawn from the same source." The trip had changed him. He felt that it had turned him from a boy into a man. The loneliness and mystery of the Arctic and the feelings it had inspired stimulated his imagination. "It is a region of purity, of white ice and of blue water, with no human dwelling within a thousand miles to sully the freshness of the breeze which blows across the icefields," he wrote. "And then it is a region of romance also. You stand on the very brink of the unknown. . . . If you have once been there, the thought of it haunts you all your life."

After his months in the Arctic, the last term of medical school was not much of a challenge. In 1881, he became a Bachelor of Medicine and a Master of Surgery. He eagerly accepted an offer to serve as ship's surgeon again, this time on the *Mayumba,* a steamer bound for the west coast of Africa, leaving on October 22. There were several passengers on board, and he was employed to care for their health. In contrast to his experience on the *Hope,* on the *Mayumba* there was actually some call for Conan Doyle's medical services, but he was not wholly successful as a doctor. He wrote to his mother, "There is a frightful horror (Mrs. McSomething) going to Madeira for her lungs. . . . She won't let me examine her chest. 'Young doctors take such liberties, you know my dear'—so I have washed my hands of her." But soon he had enough work without worrying about Mrs. McSomething, because everyone aboard became seasick.

As he had on the *Hope,* Conan Doyle sought out as much adventure as possible. He swam all around the ship in shark-infested waters—just to prove that he could. "Several times I have done utterly reckless things with so little motive that I have found it difficult to explain them to myself afterwards," he remarked in his autobiography. "This was one of them." He took a canoe up the Old Calabar River, encountering crocodiles, poisonous snakes, and flesh-eating fish.

But he did not enjoy this voyage as he had the previous one. He had loved the Arctic cold, whereas he hated the African climate. The heat bothered him, and in Lagos he caught a fever from which, because he was the only doctor around who could have treated it, he almost died. (While he was sick, another passenger died of the same fever.) Although he admired a few places, and was excited to see a blue butterfly so large he thought it was a bird, most of Africa repelled him. The area around the Old Calabar River he described as a kind of hell: "Dark and terrible mangrove swamps lay on either side with gloomy shades where nothing that is not horrible could exist. It is indeed a foul place." The Bonny River in Lagos was, he said, despite its name, "in all ways hateful with its brown smelling stream and its mango swamps."

The voyage continued ill-fated to the end. On the way back, a slow fire started in the bunkers right next to the ship's cargo of oil. For the first few days the fire smoldered more or less under control, but on the fourth day, near Portugal, it blazed up so that the iron sides of the ship grew red-hot. It seemed that they might have to take to the lifeboats, and Conan Doyle imagined himself showing up as a castaway in Lisbon to surprise his sister, who was working there as a governess. However, the fire was brought back under control, and the ship limped back into Liverpool harbor on January 14, 1882. Conan Doyle wrote cheerfully to the Ma'am, "Just a line, to say that I have turned up all safe after having had the African fever, been nearly eaten by a shark, and as a finale the *Mayumba* catching fire between Madeira and England."

Dr. Arthur Conan Doyle in his academic robes at the time he received his medical degree.

"A Capricious Creature Who Frequently Growls"

Standing on the deck of the *Mayumba* in a raging storm, Conan Doyle had considered his future and decided that this would be his last sea voyage. Despite the sharks, fevers, and fires, his reason was that life as a ship's doctor was too easy. He believed that "one or two more such voyages would sap my simple habits and make me unfit for the hard struggle which any sort of success would need."

With no money to buy a medical practice (as was customary at the time), and no contacts to help him get started, he had a difficult road ahead. Now the fame and influence of the Doyle family could be of real use to him. He was summoned to London to face the family council. They were not in a position to help him financially, his aunts and uncles told him, but they would be happy to recommend him as a doctor to important Catholic authorities. With a few well-placed words, he could count on having most of the Catholic community anywhere he wished as his patients. Now Conan Doyle faced a moral dilemma. If he accepted this offer, he could easily set himself up anywhere in England and be confident of success. But he had ceased to accept the Catholic religion, and he was too honest to benefit from a falsehood. He told his aunts and uncles that he could not allow himself to be represented as a believer in the Catholic Church. He was an agnostic, he explained— he believed that the mysteries of the spiritual world were outside the realm of human comprehension.

The family was appalled. The Doyles had a long, proud history of standing up for their faith. Most of the family fortune and land had been lost during the Reformation, when the Doyles had refused to convert to Protestantism. More recently, Arthur's uncle Richard had resigned in protest from his highly placed position at the influential *Punch* magazine when *Punch* had ridiculed the pope. The Doyle family urged Arthur to reconsider, and when he tried to explain his position to them he got excited and argued so fiercely that he offended them deeply. He believed that it was impossible to stay within the Church and maintain his intellectual self-respect. His relatives were too fond of him to cast him out completely, but they felt they could no longer offer him any help. He was on his own.

Arthur's loss of religious faith had started when what seemed to him the harsh and narrow-minded attitudes of the Jesuits at Stonyhurst began to trouble him. "Even as a boy, all that was sanest and most generous in my nature rose up against a narrow theology and an uncharitable outlook upon the other religions of the world," he wrote in *Memories and Adventures*. He remembered all his life the moment he realized he could no longer accept the Jesuits' teachings. "I heard Father Murphy, a great fierce Irish priest, declare that there was sure damnation for everyone outside the Church. I looked upon him with horror, and to that moment I traced the first rift which has grown into such a chasm between me and those who were my guides." The suffering and disease he encountered in medical school further weakened his ability to believe in the divine, benevolent God of Christianity. If God existed, then it was he who created the horrible illnesses that destroyed innocent people. Conan Doyle wrote of a god who

> . . . chokes the infant throat with slime,
> He sets the ferment free;
> He builds the tiny tube of lime
> That blocks the artery.

The evidence of his own eyes seemed to refute the religious beliefs of his family.

Without the belief in which he had been raised, he felt "as if my life-belt had burst." He needed something to believe in, and in college, the exciting new theories of the leading thinkers of the time—John Stuart Mill, Thomas Huxley, Charles Darwin—who substituted reason and scientific method for blind faith, offered him an alternative. He became a materialist, abandoning belief in the idea of an immortal soul, and took up the scientific attitude that would guide his life from that time on: "Never will I accept anything which cannot be proved to me. The evils of religion have all come from accepting things which cannot be proved." He still retained the spiritual reverence for life that the Arctic had awakened in him, however. He did not doubt that some great spiritual and moral truth existed that should guide human life. He began his long search for a philosophy of life that could be tested and proved, yet still had a place in it for the Divine.

Arthur left his Doyle uncles' household with his spiritual integrity and self-respect intact, but penniless and with no prospects. At exactly the right moment, he received an invitation from a college friend, Dr. George Budd, a loud, manic, imaginative character whom Conan Doyle found attractive, stimulating, and somewhat overwhelming. Even though the two men had sometimes come to blows, life was never dull around Budd. "He is one of those men who make a kind of magnetic atmosphere, so that you feel exhilarated and stimulated in their presence," Conan Doyle wrote. In college, Budd had been a champion rugby player and was noted for his wild plans and inventions.

Now Budd wanted Conan Doyle to join him in his practice at Plymouth. When Conan Doyle wrote with some practical questions, Budd telegrammed back with characteristic bluster: WHY NOT CALL ME A LIAR AT ONCE? I TELL YOU I HAVE SEEN THIRTY THOUSAND PATIENTS IN THE LAST YEAR. . . . ALL PATIENTS COME TO ME. WOULD NOT CROSS THE STREET TO SEE QUEEN VICTORIA. . . . WILL GUARANTEE THREE HUNDRED POUNDS FIRST YEAR. Conan Doyle's mother mistrusted Budd, and advised him not to go, but this seemed too good an offer to turn down, and for one of the few times in his life, Conan Doyle ignored his mother's advice.

At Plymouth, Conan Doyle found that Budd really had built up a practice as good as he claimed. Conan Doyle was fascinated and somewhat repelled by his methods, but had to admit they were effective. Budd offered free consultations, in order to lure patients in. Then he prescribed heroic doses of medicine, for which he charged heavily. He despised the standard ideals of professional courtesy and the kindly, soothing family doctor. "The more difficulties you throw in the way [of your patients] the more they think of it," he advised Conan Doyle. "Break your patients in early, and keep them to heel." Budd bullied his patients, shouting at them, scolding them, and mesmerizing them with the strength of

Dr. Cullingworth from The Stark Munro Letters, *a transparently fictionalized version of his college friend Dr. Budd. Conan Doyle describes him as "well-grown . . . with square shoulders, an arching chest, and a quick jerky way of walking. . . . His face was wonderfully ugly."*

From *The Stark Munro Letters*

Although this description of the bizarre methods of Dr. Cullingworth comes from The Stark Munro Letters, *a work of fiction Conan Doyle wrote many years after his time in Portsmouth, the author said that Cullingworth was an accurate picture of Dr. George Budd and that the incidents described are true. Despite the bitter rift that would develop between Conan Doyle and Budd, a certain amused affection can be sensed in Doyle's portrait, and there is clearly some commonsense behind Budd's antics.*

It is impossible for me to give you any idea of that long line of patients, filing hour after hour through the unfurnished room, and departing, some amused, and some frightened, with their labels in their hands. Cullingworth's antics are beyond belief. I laughed until I thought the wooden chair under me would have come to pieces. He roared, he raved, he swore, he pushed them about, slapped them on the back, shoved them against the wall, and occasionally rushed out to the head of the stair to address them en masse. At the same time, behind all this tomfoolery, I, watching his prescriptions, could see a quickness of diagnosis, a scientific insight, and a daring and unconventional use of drugs, which satisfied me that he was right in saying that, under all this charlatanism, there lay solid reasons for his success. Indeed, "charlatanism" is a misapplied word in this connection; for it would describe the doctor who puts on an artificial and conventional manner with his patients, rather than one who is absolutely frank and true to his own extraordinary nature.

To some of his patients he neither said one word nor did he allow them to say one. With a loud "hush" he would rush at them, thump them on the chests, listen to their hearts, write their labels, and then run them out of the room by their shoulders. One poor old lady he

text continues on page 42

text continued from page 41

greeted with a perfect scream. "You've been drinking too much tea!" he cried. "You are suffering from tea poisoning!" Then, without allowing her to get a word in, he clutched her by her crackling black mantle, dragged her up to the table, and held out a copy of "Taylor's Medical Jurisprudence" which was lying there. "Put your hand on the book," he thundered, "and swear that for fourteen days you will drink nothing but cocoa." She swore with upturned eyes, and was instantly whirled off with her label in her hand, to the dispensary. I could imagine that to the last day of her life, the old lady would talk of her interview with Cullingworth; and I could well understand how the village from which she came would send fresh recruits to block up his waiting rooms.

Another portly person was seized by the two armholes of his waist-coat, just as he was opening his mouth to explain his symptoms, and was rushed backward down the passage, down the stairs, and finally into the street, to the immense delight of the assembled patients, "You eat too much, drink too much, and sleep too much," Cullingworth roared after him. "Knock down a policeman, and come again when they let you out." Another patient complained of a "sinking feeling." "My dear," said he, "take your medicine; and if that does no good, swallow the cork, for there is nothing better when you are sinking."

As far as I could judge, the bulk of the patients looked upon a morning at Cullingworth's as a most enthralling public entertainment, tempered only by a thrill lest it should be their turn next to be made an exhibition of.

his personality. He ran out of his office to stand on the landing of the stairs and shout insults at the crowd below. He made old ladies swear on one of his medical books never to touch tea again. "A morning with him when the practice was in full blast was as funny as any pantomime and I was exhausted with laughter," Conan Doyle wrote.

Budd had brought about some dramatic cures, largely by telling the patients so forcefully that he had solved their problem that they did not dare not to recover, but also, as Conan Doyle saw, because he was, underneath all his dramatics, an excellent diagnostician. Patients came from miles around to see him. Every room of Budd's house, as well as the stable, was packed with waiting patients. Sometimes Budd would consent to see them; sometimes he would suddenly decide to take a break and people who had waited for hours would be sent home to return the next day and wait some more. At the end of the day, Budd and his wife would parade through the streets displaying the large bag of money they had taken in that day, making sure to walk past the windows of all the conventional doctors of Plymouth who, of course, scorned Budd's methods. "They all come to their windows and gnash their teeth and dance until I am out of sight," he gloated to Conan Doyle.

Amused and skeptical, Conan Doyle settled into Budd's household. He respected Budd, despite his theatrics, yet realized he was "a capricious creature who frequently growls and may possibly bite." At first, the practice neither fulfilled Conan Doyle's high hopes nor justified his mother's fears. Budd sent a trickle of patients across the hall to Conan Doyle's office, but Conan Doyle could not bring himself to adopt Budd's aggressive conduct, and the patients found him bland. His mother, to whom he wrote often, continued to be hostile to Budd, especially when she heard that Budd had left his previous practice at Bristol without paying his debts. She wrote to her son urging him to get away, but in his responses he always loyally defended Budd, whatever his private doubts.

Then one day Budd came to Conan Doyle and told him he was ruining the practice. Budd did not blame him—it was just that the patients all wanted to see Dr. Budd, not Dr. Doyle. When they saw two doctors' names on the door, he explained, some of them worried that they might be shown into the wrong man's office, so they stopped coming altogether. Conan Doyle's reaction was characteristic and decisive. He marched downstairs, seized a hammer, and ripped his brass nameplate from the door. "That won't interfere with you any more," he told Budd.

Budd said he felt a responsibility to the younger doctor. After all, Conan Doyle had turned down other jobs to work with him and he had not earned the promised 300 pounds a year. So Budd offered to help him set up as a doctor elsewhere. He would send a pound every week to help support him while he built a practice of his own. With no particular reason to go any one place or another, Conan Doyle settled on Southsea, the residential district of Portsmouth. This was a small, pleasant city similar to Plymouth, and as a port it would be full of sailors who would remind him of his happy times at sea. With a few pounds in his pocket and the promise of a regular income from Budd, he set off in July 1882, not unhappily, "with one small trunk containing all my earthly possessions, to start practice in a town in which I knew no single soul."

Conan Doyle did not even know where to look for his first night's lodging, so he just got on a streetcar and asked the conductor to let him off somewhere near a cheap lodging house. That evening he went for a stroll around the shabby neighborhood to which the conductor had directed him. Remembering the image he wished to project, of a trustworthy doctor, he dressed carefully in his frock coat, gloves, and top hat. In the street he passed a drunken man who was kicking his wife, and reacted as usual, plowing in to the rescue of the lady, gloves and all. The watching crowd, seeing a very large, well-dressed man attacking a smaller working-class man, immediately came to the drunken husband's defense, and a brawl developed. Because a blow aimed at Conan Doyle hit a nearby soldier instead, he was able to slip away while the soldier took his place in the fight—otherwise he might have spent his first night in Southsea in jail.

The next day he set about finding a place to live and work. He proceeded methodically. Tramping through every street in Portsmouth with a map, he marked down every doctor's office and every vacant house. Then he chose a house not near too many doctors, at a busy crossroads, and close to an inn and a church. Gleefully he entered the first house he could call his own, where he would be responsible to no one but himself, thinking, "It is a wonderful thing to have a house of your own for the first time, however humble it may be."

He walked right into a pile of grinning teeth. After a startled moment, he realized that the last inhabitant must have been a dentist who used the teeth as models. Other than these, and a single chest, the house was empty. With his last remaining money, he bought furniture for his waiting room and the consulting room where he would see patients. To the public, his house would seem completely furnished—they would not see that he had been unable to afford any furniture for himself. He had a bed frame, but no mattress or blankets, and the kitchen contained only a trunk that he used as a place to store his food, as a table, and as a chair. He cooked by hanging his kettle over the gas jet. The rest would have to wait.

He now had only a few pennies left to live on until he could attract his first patients, but with his natural optimism, he was not worried. He crept out after dark to shine the brass plate with his name, to conceal the fact that he could not afford a servant. He managed to obtain a supply of drugs on credit, and he believed he could earn enough

This brass nameplate is probably the one Conan Doyle ripped from Dr. Budd's door in anger, and the one he crept down to polish at night in Southsea so that no one would see he could not afford to pay a servant to do it for him.

to pay for the drugs and the rent by the time they came due. He figured he could feed himself on a diet of bread, tea, milk, sausages, and American tinned beef cheaply enough to hold out, as long as he had Budd's one pound a week to live on. So he wrote to Budd that he had established himself in Bush Villas, and settled back to starve while he waited for his pound to arrive.

Instead he received a letter that solved the mystery of Budd's sudden decision to throw him out. Budd wrote that after Conan Doyle had left, the servant girl had come to him with the scraps of some letters that she had found in the fireplace. He had carefully glued these pieces together—and discovered, to his horror, that Conan Doyle had been carrying on an abusive correspondence about him with the Ma'am all the time Budd was employing him. In the letter he had found, he said, Conan Doyle's mother had called him, "a man of unscrupulous character and doubtful antecedents," and "a bankrupt swindler." Indignantly, Budd declared that he owed nothing to such a treacherous deceiver and would send him no money.

Conan Doyle's first reaction was that Budd was being unfair. It was true that the Ma'am had been criticizing Budd in her letters, but that was because Conan Doyle had been defending him. Then something even stranger about Budd's story occurred to him. Conan Doyle never threw his mother's letters away. He kept them. Usually he just stuck them into his pocket until it got too full to hold any more. In fact, when he checked, he discovered that the letter Budd quoted was in his pocket at that very moment. Budd could not have found any scraps to piece together—he must have been reading Conan Doyle's letters all along while Conan Doyle was still living there. Instead of confronting him at the time, though, Budd had kicked him out with a promise of financial help he had never intended to keep. Then he had strung him along pretending to be friendly until Conan Doyle had committed himself financially. Only when he thought Conan Doyle would be ruined had he revealed his anger.

Conan Doyle wrote him a scathing letter, thanking him. Budd had done him two favors, he said: He had removed the only source of conflict between Conan Doyle and his mother, because now he could agree with her that Budd was an unscrupulous swindler; and he had pushed Conan Doyle into starting his own practice, which turned out to be exactly what he wanted to do anyway.

Years later Conan Doyle got his revenge on Budd in his hilarious novel *The Stark Munro Letters,* which tells the story of their venture together, lightly fictionalized. Budd appears as Dr. Cullingworth, and Conan Doyle is Stark Munro. Having immortalized Budd as a strange half-mad genius and buffoon and ensured that it would be his own version of the story that the public heard, Conan Doyle could afford to be generous and forgive Budd. "I have no doubt he did a great deal of good, for there was reason and knowledge behind all that he did," Conan Doyle admits in *Memories and Adventures,* and "He had, of course, no real grievance, but I am quite willing to admit that he honestly thought he had." All in all, said Conan Doyle, "I liked him and even now I can't help liking him."

Mary Doyle, Arthur Conan Doyle's mother, in her early fifties. She was devoted to her son and passed on to him her love of reading. He remembered that as a child he watched her stir the porridge with one hand while using the other to hold her book.

One Bush Villas in Southsea, the site of Conan Doyle's first practice, where the first Sherlock Holmes story was written. Conan Doyle is standing to the left of the entrance, near the red lamp that indicated a doctor's office. His brass nameplate is attached to the railing at his right.

DR. CONAN DOYLE OF BUSH VILLAS

Now young Dr. Conan Doyle had nothing to do but sit and wait for someone to knock on his door. Finally, a man with a cough showed up at the door, but just as Conan Doyle was preparing to diagnose bronchitis, the man revealed that he was only calling to collect for a balance left on the gas bill by the previous tenant. No one else came. "It used to amuse me to sit upstairs and count how many of the passersby stopped to look at my plate," Conan Doyle recalled. "This used to cheer me up and make me feel that something was going on." All through a beautiful autumn, he sat in his consulting room the entire day, hoping for patients. Such inactivity was difficult for someone used to an energetic life. "At night when all hope of patients was gone for that day I would lock up my house and walk many miles to work off my energy," he remembered. Often he did not get home until dawn.

Eventually a very few poor people in the neighborhood came, and one hypochondriac who was making the rounds of all the doctors in town. Conan Doyle happened to be shopping at a local store when the grocer collapsed in an epileptic seizure, and they worked out an agreement whereby Conan Doyle would treat him in return for groceries. He felt rather ghoulish waiting hopefully for the grocer to have another fit, but at least it kept him from starvation. Obviously just waiting for patients to come was not enough. He had to *do* something.

One possibility quickly presented itself. Arthur's uncle Richard, who was a very kind man, was unhappy at the breach between them and sent him, unasked, a letter of introduction to the Southsea Catholic bishop. But even in his current precarious position, Conan Doyle would not compromise his principles. "It seemed to me that it would be playing it rather low down to use a religious organisation to my own advantage, when I condemned them in the abstract," he wrote. To avoid temptation, he burned the letter.

Now some of Dr. Budd's advice came to mind. After all, whatever else could be said about Budd, he certainly knew how to attract attention. Budd said that it always helped to get your name in the newspapers. Doctors did not advertise, but Conan Doyle took out a notice announcing that Dr. Arthur Conan Doyle had moved to Bush Villas, and hoped that people might think he had come from an established practice elsewhere.

Then he had a stroke of luck—a gentleman suffered a riding accident right in front of his door. After caring for him, Conan Doyle went down to the office of the *Evening News* to tell them of the incident, and that evening a paragraph reported that the injured lawyer "was conveyed into the house of Dr. Conan Doyle of Bush Villas, and that gentleman was able to pronounce that, although considerably shaken and bruised, there was no injury of any consequence." Conan Doyle's account of the incident to his former employer Dr. Hoare was somewhat more flippant. "A man had the good taste to fall off his horse the other day just in front of the window," he wrote, "and the intelligent animal rolled on him. I stuck him together again, and it got into all the papers and got my name known a little."

Knowing no one, and sitting all day in his consulting room, Conan Doyle became very lonely. And he was concerned that it did not look good for him to open the door to patients himself. A doctor was supposed to have a servant. As soon as he had enough patients to be sure he was not going to starve, he wrote to his mother asking if his little brother, Innes, who was 10, could come keep house for him. Innes's arrival helped considerably. He was cheerful, energetic, and excellent company. He was also an incurable optimist. Shortly after he arrived, he wrote their mother, "The patients are crowding in. We have made three bob this week. We have vaxenated a baby and got hold of a man with consumtion, and to-day a gipsy's cart came up to the door. . . . We found out that the gipsy's child had measles. . . . After all we got sixpence out of them and that is all ways something." Actually, according to Arthur, he had ended up *giving* the gypsies sixpence before they would leave. "A few more such patients and I am a broken man," he wrote.

Finally Conan Doyle realized that sitting all day waiting was not very useful. He had been afraid to leave his office, in case some patient came while he was gone. Now he followed his naturally sociable instincts and took the risk. If anyone did show up, Innes could run out and find him. He joined the Southsea Bowling Club and the North End Cricket Club, and started playing rugby. To establish himself among the more educated society of Southsea he joined the Literary and Scientific Society. These tactics paid off. Not only was he much happier with more human contact, but because people tended to like and trust Conan Doyle once they knew him, his practice grew. One of the men at the bowling club was the superintendent of an insurance company, and he arranged for Conan Doyle to become the company's medical authority. He became the regular physician of a dignified elderly lady who periodically "went on a wild burst, in the course of which she would skim plates out of the window at the passers-by." Other references followed, and Conan Doyle also found part-time work at a nearby eye hospital.

Although his earnings were enough to survive on, they were not much more than that. That first year, he earned only 154 pounds. He filled out his income tax form, indicating that he had not earned enough to pay any taxes. It was returned to him by a skeptical examiner with "This is most unsatisfactory" written across the top. He wrote back, "I entirely agree."

Slowly his practice increased, and by his third year he was making 300 pounds a year, as much as his father had ever earned. In his eight years in Portsmouth, his income never passed this mark. He quickly became a well-known citizen of the town. He was the captain of the cricket club, and his sporting successes were frequently reported in the papers. The lectures of the literary society became a regular part of his life, and it was here that he picked up much of the miscellaneous knowledge Sherlock Holmes would later exhibit.

At first, Conan Doyle felt too shy to participate in the debates that followed the lectures. Before he spoke he trembled so much that he claimed everyone on the bench with him could feel it shake. Finally he conquered his shyness enough to give some lectures himself. His first lecture was on his experiences in the Arctic. To illustrate it, he borrowed so many stuffed animal specimens that he left the audience with the impression that he was a great game hunter. He also lectured on historian Edward Gibbon, author of *The Decline and Fall of the Roman Empire,* and on his hero, social historian Thomas Carlyle. He was eventually elected secretary of the society. Starting from nothing, he had successfully built a life for himself. As a Portsmouth newspaper commented, "Considering the comparatively short time he has been amongst us, his tall, athletic, broad-shouldered figure is extremely familiar to a large number of Portsmouth people."

One of his patients was Major General Alfred W. Drayson, a soldier, author, astronomy professor, and committed believer in spiritualism. Drayson became a friend, and, with his encouragement, Conan Doyle began to explore various aspects of the supernatural. He experimented with communication by mental telepathy with a friend. "Again and again," he reported, "sitting behind him, I have drawn diagrams, and he in turn has made approximately the same figure." He attended several spirit drawing sessions and seances where the sitters asked questions and were answered by the tapping of a table leg that spelled out the replies. Some of the answers impressed him; still his conclusion was that probably "we were collectively pushing the table."

Even when he could come up with no rational explanation for the strange events he witnessed at a seance, Conan Doyle was sometimes troubled by the seemingly trivial and foolish nature of the messages received from the spirits. Why would someone come back from the dead in order to shake a tambourine or blow a horn? One medium, Mrs. Maggs, called forth showers of eggs, fruits, and vegetables, which, she said, were gifts from a spiritualist circle in Brooklyn, New York. (The same Brooklyn group also sent a flock of pigeons that left very unspiritual droppings in the room.) The best explanation he could come up with was that the spirits' manifestations were like the ring of a telephone—insignificant in themselves and only meant to indicate that there was someone there with a message.

Spiritualism attracted and fascinated Conan Doyle, but he still felt "the usual contempt which the young educated man feels towards the whole subject which has been covered by the clumsy name of spiritualism." Although he wanted to, he was not able to believe in the existence of a soul separate from the body. All his medical experience kept

Louise Hawkins, Conan Doyle's first wife. He was probably thinking of her when he described Mary Morstan, Watson's first wife, in The Sign of the Four: *"Her expression was sweet and amiable, and her large blue eyes were singularly spiritual and sympathetic. . . . I have never looked upon a face which gave a clearer promise of a refined and sensitive nature."*

forcing him to the conclusion that the mind was "an emanation from the brain and entirely physical in its nature. I saw, as a medical man, how a spicule of bone or a tumour pressing on the brain would cause what seemed an alteration in the soul. . . . The physical argument seemed an overpowering one." Still, he continued to attend spiritualist gatherings and read everything he could, and he tried to keep an open mind.

A friend of Conan Doyle's, Dr. William Pike, called him in for a consultation about a young patient named Jack Hawkins. After examining him, Conan Doyle realized that Jack had cerebral meningitis and there was nothing that could be done for him. The boy was living in lodgings with his mother and his sister, Louise (or Louisa), but because of the seizures his disease caused, the owner of their boardinghouse would not let them stay. They had nowhere else to go, and Pike, knowing Conan Doyle could use the extra money, proposed that they move into Conan Doyle's house, where Jack could be treated as a resident patient. A few days later, Jack Hawkins died. There was nothing Conan Doyle could have done, but he worried that a hearse departing from his front door was not the kind of advertisement Dr. Budd would have recommended. However, this incident also had a more pleasing result.

Now that he was comfortably settled, Conan Doyle had begun to think about marriage. He had already courted several girls—one named Elmo Weldon fairly seriously—and had been flirting a lot. "I went to a ball the other night," he wrote to his sister Lottie, "and by some mischance got as drunk as an owl. I have a dim recollection that I proposed to half the women in the room—married and single. I got one letter next day signed 'Ruby,' and saying the writer had said 'yes' when she meant 'no'; but who the deuce she was or what she had said 'yes' about I can't conceive." Louise Hawkins was now resident in his house, and he had seen much to admire while he watched her tend her brother. Within a month they were engaged, and soon after, in 1885, they were married.

Conan Doyle was very fond of his wife, whom he called "Touie," and she was devoted to him. She was a sympathetic, self-effacing woman with, as her daughter later wrote, "a gentle all-lovingness about her that drew the simple folk, children, and animals to her, as to a magnet," and had "a bright ripple of fun." Conan Doyle described her as "a very gentle and amiable girl," and said, "no one could have had a more gentle and amiable companion." These two adjectives seem to sum up his view of her. In descriptions from people who knew them both, his strong personality completely overwhelms hers, and in his own autobiography, he never once mentions her by name. Still, she filled an important place in his life. These were very happy years for Conan Doyle. He had a position in life, an adequate income, and a wife to care for and to make him comfortable. He settled happily into the existence of a locally prominent gentleman doctor who wrote a little on the side.

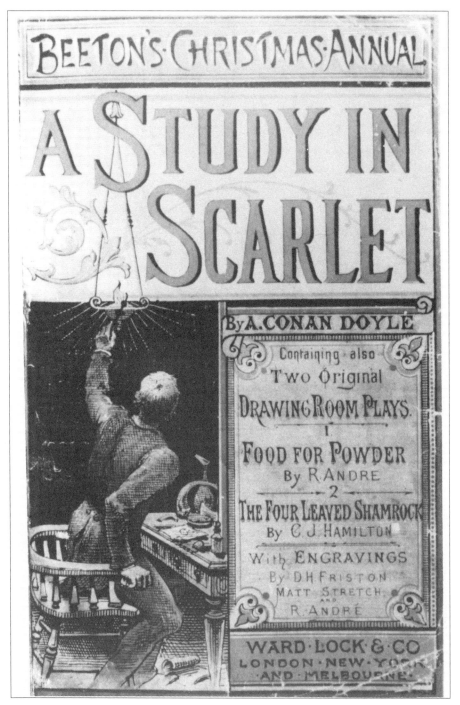

Sherlock Holmes's first appearance in print, in 1887. The publisher's advertisement claimed, "Every detective ought to read 'A Study in Scarlet' as a most helpful means to his own advancement. . . . 'A Study in Scarlet' should be the talk of every Christmas gathering throughout the land."

"Feeling Large Thoughts Rise Within Me"

Conan Doyle had never given up his writing, but he did not expect it to be more than a sideline. When he outlined his future for his mother, he included among the talk of good hospitals and honorary surgeonships his intention to "supplement my income by literature." He had been writing an occasional short story and had published about a dozen in journals such as *London Society* and the *Boy's Own Paper,* but he did not take them seriously. He dismissed them in *Memories and Adventures* with the comment, "They served their purpose in relieving me of a little of that financial burden which always pressed upon me."

Now he found that married life, which provided a sympathetic listener to discuss things with and read aloud to, stimulated his creativity. "My brain seems to have quickened and both my imagination and my range of expression were greatly improved," he wrote. He began to write stories he was proud of. He drew on his unusual experiences for settings, placing his stories on Arctic whalers and in Africa. His subject matter tended toward the uncanny: ghosts, mummies, and supernatural relics.

His first real success came when "J. Habakuk Jephson's

Statement" was accepted by *Cornhill Magazine*. Not only was this prestigious journal the publisher of Robert Louis Stevenson and William Makepeace Thackeray, it paid him 29 guineas—almost a full year's rent. The story offers an explanation for the strange, true incident of the *Mary Celeste,* a ship that was found adrift near the Azores, fully seaworthy, with food and water in the hold, all the men's clothing and pipes still in their sea chests, an impression still visible in the bedding where the captain's baby daughter had slept, and the entire crew mysteriously missing. Conan Doyle's story describes a rebellion led by a black passenger and several black sailors, who divert the ship to Africa, slay all the white crew, and vanish into the African desert. Conan Doyle presents a crudely caricatured view of the African natives, but he does try to present both sides of the case.

The story attracted various sorts of attention. One review began, "*Cornhill Magazine* opens its new number with a story which would have made Thackeray turn in his grave." More flatteringly, another reviewer concluded that the story, which was published anonymously, must have been written by Robert Louis Stevenson, one of the most admired writer of the time.

Perhaps the most gratifying response of all to "J. Habakuk Jephson's Statement" came not from literary critics but from Frederick Solly Flood, Her Majesty's Proctor and Attorney General at Gibraltar, who had been in charge of the salvage of the *Mary Celeste.* This gentleman reported to the government that Dr. J. Habakuk Jephson's statement was "a fabrication from beginning to end," and the doctor should not have been allowed to publish such a false account that might harm England's relations with other countries. Meanwhile, U.S. consul Horatio J. Sprague was asking *Cornhill Magazine* to look into the origins of this fraudulent article. For the first time—but not the last—Conan Doyle had presented an implausible story with such convincing trappings of realism that his fiction was mistaken for a genuine report.

Happy though he was at the favorable attention his story received, Conan Doyle was beginning to chafe against the tradition of publishing magazine stories anonymously. "It was great praise," he explained, "but something less warm, which came straight to my own address, would have pleased me better." He decided it was time to publish a novel, with his name on the cover. His first effort, with the unpromisingly ordinary name *The Narrative of John Smith,* was lost in the mail the first time he sent it out to a publisher. Little is known about it, except for Conan Doyle's later comment that "my shock at its disappearance would be as nothing to my horror if it were suddenly to appear again—in print." His second attempt, called *Girdlestone & Co.,* struck him even as he was writing it as dull and derivative, so he was not surprised when he could not interest anyone. "When I sent it to publishers and they scorned it I quite acquiesced in their decision." Like most first novels, both of these manuscripts were heavily autobiographical. For his third attempt he decided to try something different.

He remembered how much he had loved Edgar Allan Poe's stories of the detective C. Auguste Dupin—considered the first true detective stories—and had admired the "neat dovetailing" of the plot in Émile Gaboriau's classic mysteries about his detective, Lecoq. All fictional detectives since these two, Conan Doyle felt, had been inept, the stories relying for their solutions on coincidence or melodrama, rather than intelligent reasoning. Perhaps he could do better.

He hoped to describe a system by which mysteries could be solved using only the clues given and the inspired application of logic—what he called "an exact science" of detection. It is easy to forget that when Conan Doyle was dreaming up Sherlock Holmes, there was no such system. The first textbook attempting to organize what was known about footprints and fingerprints, bloodstains and criminal types, Dr. Hans Cross's *Criminal Investigation,* would not be published until 1891, four years after Sherlock Holmes first appeared, and it did not appear in English until 1906. Creating the science of detection was an interesting challenge, but Conan Doyle's main purpose was, as always, to tell a good story that would haunt the reader. The problem was how, without convenient confessions, stock villains, and melodramatic midnight abductions, to write something about close reasoning that was not just a dull exercise in logic.

Some preliminary scribbles in his notebook have survived. A title: "A Tangled Skein." A false start: "The terrified woman rushing up to the cabman. The two going in search of a policeman. John Reeves had been 7 years in the force; John Reeves went back with them." A name for the narrator: "Ormond Sacker." And a name for the detective: "Sherringford Holmes."

The breakthrough came when Conan Doyle remembered how fascinated he had been watching his former teacher Dr. Joseph Bell lean back with his fingers together and tell his patients all about themselves using "his eerie trick of spotting details." He would use Bell's brilliant deductions and showmanship as the starting point. He also borrowed (and exaggerated) Bell's tall, lean physique and eager, razor-sharp face for his detective. After this inspiration, the writing of *A Study in Scarlet* came easily. The entire novel took him only three months to write.

A Study in Scarlet begins with Dr. John Watson's brief account of his early life setting up a not-particularly-successful medical practice and going abroad as an army doctor. His story is similar to Conan Doyle's own. Watson, who is looking for an apartment mate to share expenses, is introduced to an eccentric character with a flat to share at 221B Baker Street. With his now famous first words to the astonished Watson, "You have been in Afghanistan, I perceive,"

● Study in Scarlet

Ormond Sacker - ~~from South~~ from Afghanistan
 Lived at 221 B Upper Baker Street
with
 I Sherrinford Holmes -
   The Laws of Evidence
 Reserved -
Sleepy eyed young man - philosopher - Collector of rare Violins.
An Amati -
      Chemical laboratory
  I have four hundred a year -
I am a Consulting detective -
What rot this is" I cried - throwing the volume
: petulantly aside " I must say that I have no
patience with people who build up fine theories in their
own armchairs which can never be reduced to
practice -
   Lecoq was a bungler -
Dupin was better. Dupin was decidedly smart -
His trick of following a train of thought was more
sensational than clever but still he had analytical genius.

Conan Doyle's early notes from the composition of A Study in Scarlet. At the bottom of the page can be seen Sherlock Holmes's criticisms of Lecoq and Dupin, two of Conan Doyle's models for Holmes. The opinions expressed are Holmes's, not the author's.

Sherlock Holmes claimed the spotlight that he still holds today.

Holmes, who is in the process of establishing himself as the world's first "consulting detective," is invited by an acquaintance at Scotland Yard to assist in investigating the unexplained murder of an American named Enoch Drebber. He unravels a complicated chain of events leading back to the early Mormon settlements in Utah. One half of the book, in which Holmes does not even appear, is taken up with the romantic and sensationalistic story of the tragic love affair in Utah that would eventually lead to the murder in London, and the other half details how Holmes works out this story years later and half the world away.

With *A Study in Scarlet,* Conan Doyle could tell he had succeeded. "I knew that the book was as good as I could make it, and I had high hopes. When . . . my little Holmes book began to do the circular tour [from publisher to publisher] I was hurt, for I knew that it deserved a better fate." Most publishers, assuming that it was just another so-called shilling dreadful—the kind of gory adventure-mystery to which Conan Doyle was trying to provide an alternative— did not even bother reading it.

Finally, the editor at Ward, Lock & Co., G. T. Bettany, gave it to his wife to read. Jeannie Gwynne Bettany, herself a writer, reported, "This man is a born novelist. It will be a great success!" Bettany was dubious, but decided to make Conan Doyle an offer. "We have read your story and are pleased with it," he wrote with no particular enthusiasm. They would not want to publish it in 1886 because "the market is flooded at present with cheap fiction," but if he was willing to wait until next year, they could offer Conan Doyle 25 pounds for it. They would own the copyright and would not pay royalties. This was not a very inviting offer, but it was better than nothing, and Conan Doyle was tired of sending his manuscript out, so he accepted. That 25 pounds was all he ever received for the first appearance of his famous character.

When the book appeared a year later, it was not published by itself, but as the main story in *Beeton's Christmas Annual* for 1887. It did not attract much attention, but it was well reviewed. The *Scotsman* said, "This is as entrancing a tale of ingenuity in tracing out crime, as has been written since the time of Edgar Allan Poe. The author shows genius. He has not trodden in the well-worn paths." The *Hampshire Post* said, "He is to be congratulated on the character of the murders, and also upon its originality." Only the review in the *Graphic* commented on the character of Sherlock

Holmes, noting that Doyle "has actually succeeded in inventing a brand new detective."

A Study in Scarlet was popular enough that when the annual sold out, the publishers reissued the mystery as a book by itself. For this edition (for which Conan Doyle received no additional payment) illustrations were commissioned from his father. Charles Doyle, who had by now been institutionalized for years and was very ill, produced some rather pathetic drawings. For his depiction of Holmes—the very first pictures of the illustrious detective—Charles used himself as a model. *A Study in Scarlet* did what Conan Doyle had wanted it to—his name had now appeared in print attached to one of his writings—and then faded away. No one realized what a phenomenon had been created, and long before it appeared, Arthur Conan Doyle

Conan Doyle writing at his desk. This picture of an earnest, prosperous, middle-class man in his solidly furnished library matches the popular conception of Dr. Watson, whom Conan Doyle clearly based, in part, on himself.

had turned his attention to other things.

While waiting for *A Study in Scarlet* to be published, Conan Doyle decided to write a more substantial book. "Having a long wait in front of me before this book could appear, and feeling large thoughts rise within me, I now determined to test my powers to the full," he explained in his autobiography. He decided to follow the example of his idol Macaulay, whose writing had brought to life for him the humanity and religious fervor of the Puritans who had fought against the supporters of the king in the English Civil War of the 1640s, and he set his novel during Monmouth's rebellion, which followed that conflict. This novel, *Micah Clarke,* in which an old man tells his adventures to his grandchildren, has not dated well. It is overly full of information from Conan Doyle's extensive research, and the self-consciously "historical" tone of the writing can become tiring. Still, as Conan Doyle said, "I fairly let myself go upon the broad highway of adventure," and it is an exciting adventure tale.

However, it was no easier to place with a publisher than his previous efforts had been. The editor of *Cornhill Magazine* rejected it with a letter, beginning, "How can you, can you, waste your time and your wits writing historical novels!" An editor at Bentley Ltd. wrote, "It lacks in our opinion the one great necessary point for fiction, i.e. interest." Finally, the manuscript was accepted by Andrew Lang at Longmans. *Micah Clarke* was well reviewed and stayed in print continuously for Conan Doyle's entire life. "It was," he wrote, "the first solid corner-stone laid for some sort of literary reputation."

While he was waiting for *Micah Clarke* to appear in print, another Conan Doyle production was also due—his first child, Mary Louise. It was a matter of suspense which would come first, but Mary Louise won. "She is fat and plump, blue eyes, bandy legs, and a fat body. Any other points will be answered on inquiry," he wrote to his mother.

"But her manners are painfully free. When she doesn't like a thing she says so, and they know it all down the street." He began his next book with the baby crawling around his feet, in sharp contrast to later life when his children regarded him with awe and would never have risked disturbing him while he was working.

His next book was another historical novel, which was in his own time considered to be his best book, and was his personal favorite. With *The White Company,* Conan Doyle went back to the historical period that most captured his imagination: the height of chivalry in the days of King Edward III of England. The story follows the adventures of a group of "manly and true" bowmen under the command of the noble Sir Nigel Loring, from the point of view of young Alleyne Edricson. For this book, published in 1890, Conan Doyle did enormous amounts of research, while still working full-time as a doctor, and it took him two laborious years. "I remember that as I wrote the last words," he says, "I felt a wave of exultation and with a cry of 'That's done it!' I hurled my inky pen across the room, where it left a black smudge upon the duck's-egg wall-paper."

Conan Doyle considered *The White Company,* along with the 1906 sequel, *Sir Nigel,* which tells of Nigel's coming-of-age quest years earlier, "the most complete, satisfying and ambitious thing that I have ever done." He wrote confidently to his sister, "I am as fond of Hordle John and Samkin Aylward and Sir Nigel Loring as though I knew them in the flesh, and I feel that the whole English-speaking race will come in time to be fond of them also." James Payn, the publisher at *Cornhill Magazine,* agreed, and so did the critics. *The White Company* went into 50 editions during Conan Doyle's lifetime alone. Although it no longer enjoys the popularity it had through the first half of the twentieth century, it is still in print.

During the two years of arduous labor it took to write *The White Company,* Conan Doyle finally found a publisher

Oscar Wilde at about the time Conan Doyle met him. His long hair and esthetic dress (including a loosely knotted ascot in place of a tie), mark Wilde as a very different kind of literary figure from Conan Doyle; however, the two men got along well and respected each other's talents.

for *Girdlestone & Co.* He also took a break to toss off another short Sherlock Holmes novel, at the request of an American publisher. Joseph Stoddart, an agent of the American firm Lippincott, had come to England looking for authors, and James Payn introduced him to Arthur Conan Doyle. Stoddart invited Conan Doyle to dinner with another author he was cultivating—Oscar Wilde.

It is hard to think of two men more different from each other than the energetic, respectable Conan Doyle and Oscar Wilde, the mannered apostle of the aesthetic movement, known as much for his velvet costumes and for strolling down the street gazing at a lily as for his elegant and opulent verse and stories. However, the dinner went well. Wilde had read and enjoyed *Micah Clarke,* and Conan Doyle found him not only brilliant and witty, but a true gentleman.

Lippincott gained two classics from this meeting, Wilde's *The Picture of Dorian Gray,* and the second Sherlock Holmes novel, *The Sign of Four* (*The Sign of the Four* in the United States), which appeared in *Lippincott's Monthly Magazine* and then in book form in 1890. This novel, involving a stolen treasure, a murderous pygmy, and a high-speed chase down the Thames River, ends with Watson marrying the client and leaving Sherlock Holmes. Clearly Conan Doyle was not intending to continue telling stories about Holmes and Watson. In England, although the book was fairly well received, it aroused no particular notice. In a typical review, the *Athenaeum* claimed, "We cannot pretend to think that *The Sign of Four* is up to the level of the writer's best work. . . . Dr. Doyle's admirers will read the little volume through eagerly enough, but they will hardly care to pick it up again."

The novel was more popular in the United States. At that time, Great Britain and the United States had no copyright agreement. This meant that once something had been published in Great Britain, any U.S. publisher was free to print it, without paying the author a penny, or even letting him know. Pirated editions of *The Sign of the Four* began to flood the United States soon after the first authorized editions appeared. Although Conan Doyle received no financial benefit from the pirated editions, their wide distribution did at least make his name—and Sherlock Holmes's—well known in the United States.

Except for a minor novel about Buddhist holy men, *The Mystery of Cloomber,* Conan Doyle produced only one other written work during his years in Southsea. This was his research thesis to earn his M.D., and it bore the unromantic title, "An Essay Upon the Vasomotor Changes in *Tabes Dorsalis* and on the Influence Which Is Exerted by the Sympathetic Nervous System in That Disease."

The famous Sidney Paget illustration showing Sherlock Holmes and Professor Moriarty locked in mortal combat at the brink of the Reichenbach Falls. Fortunately Paget did not show Holmes actually falling, thus unintentionally leaving Conan Doyle the option of bringing his detective back to life.

THE LIFE AND DEATH
OF SHERLOCK
HOLMES

After the long labor of *The White Company,* Conan Doyle was restless. His comfortably respectable provincial life was beginning to feel somewhat confining. When he heard that the German doctor Robert Koch was demonstrating what he called a sure cure for tuberculosis (perhaps the most deadly disease of Conan Doyle's time) it stirred his latent desire for escape: "A great urge came upon me suddenly that I should go to Berlin and see him do so. I could give no clear reason for this, but it was an irresistible impulse." Within a few hours he had packed his bag and left. As it turned out, it was impossible to get tickets to the demonstration at this late date, and Conan Doyle had to rely on the notes of a kindly American. He concluded, correctly, that "the whole thing was experimental and premature," and returned to Portsmouth. The entire trip took two days and accomplished nothing, but, said Conan Doyle, "I had spread my wings and had felt something of the powers within me."

On the train to Berlin, Conan Doyle became friendly with a successful London skin specialist, who had also started out as a provincial doctor. He convinced Conan Doyle to try the same path, except that since Conan Doyle had been, as he put it, amusing himself by doing a little work at the Portsmouth Eye Hospital, he would become an eye specialist. He had decided, he wrote his sister Lottie, that "I should go to London and study the eye. I should then go to Berlin and study the eye. I should then go to Paris and study the eye. Having learned all there is to know about the eye, I should come back to London and start as an eye surgeon, still, of course, keeping literature as my milch-cow."

He did not exactly follow this itinerary, but within two months he and his wife had packed up, sent their baby daughter to stay with Conan Doyle's mother, left Southsea forever, and settled in Vienna. Conan Doyle began to attend lectures there, but as he spoke only the schoolboy German he had picked up during his one year at Feldkirch, which was not up to specialized medical talk, he learned very little. Instead, he and his wife mostly socialized, going to parties and dinners, and skating. He took a little time out to write, in only 15 days, a novel about modern alchemy, *The Doings of Raffles Haw,* which paid for the trip. After several pleasant months, Conan Doyle left without earning a degree. He spent a few days in Paris with a well-known oculist, and then the Conan Doyles returned to England.

Although he scarcely qualified as a specialist, Conan Doyle moved his family to London, where he worked for a time at the Westminster Eye Clinic, and rented an office and waiting room in the fashionable medical district near Harley Street. But, as he said in *Memories and Adventures,* "I was soon to find that they were both waiting-rooms. . . . Every morning I reached my consulting-room at ten and sat there until three or four, with never a ring to disturb my serenity." The silence was depressing for a doctor, but it was the ideal setup for a writer.

At that time, the popularity of weekly and monthly literary magazines was growing rapidly. These journals drew on the new readership of commuters and day travelers that had come into being with the advent of cheap and rapid train service, and also benefited from the Victorian fondness for reading aloud at night in the family circle, just as families today watch television together. Cheaper paper and new printing techniques made such magazines inexpensive enough that they had become available to almost anyone. The pattern for the new magazines was set in the United States by such journals as *Scribner's Monthly* and *Harper's Weekly*. In England, the most successful magazine of this type was *The Strand Magazine,* which started up in 1891. Conan Doyle had published an anonymous story, "The Voice of Science," in an early edition. Now he conceived one of those brilliant ideas that seem so obvious with hindsight.

In the past, journals had mostly run long stories serialized over several months. Serials were intended for readers who subscribed to a particular journal and read it regularly; but a casual traveler who had not read the previous installments of the story would not be interested in buying a single issue. Although short stories would serve such a reader better, they did not provide a compelling reason to continue loyally buying one particular magazine every month from among the rapidly growing number of choices available. Why not, Conan Doyle thought, tell stories that were complete in themselves but featured the same character, who would draw readers back from issue to issue? This idea was not as original as Conan Doyle believed—stories with recurring characters had appeared before, most notably in Charles Dickens's *Pickwick Papers*—but Conan Doyle was the first to deliberately try to create a character whose personality would attract a regular readership.

He believed he had just such a character available, for Conan Doyle had faith in the compelling qualities of Sherlock Holmes even though the public had not yet responded. With the now celebrated opening line, "To Sherlock Holmes she is always *the* woman," he began "A

Scandal in Bohemia." Oddly enough, this story, in which Holmes is hired by the king of Bohemia to retrieve a compromising letter that could be used for blackmail, involves no real mystery. Moreover, Holmes does not succeed. He is bested by the brilliantly talented Irene Adler.

In a little more than a month, Conan Doyle had finished a second Sherlock Holmes short story and submitted both mysteries to *The Strand Magazine*. Greenough Smith, the editor, was delighted. "I realised that here was the greatest short-story writer since Edgar Allan Poe," he wrote, calling Conan Doyle's submission, "a gift from heaven, a godsend in the shape of a story that brought a gleam of happiness into the despairing life of this weary editor." He contracted for six Sherlock Holmes mysteries at 35 pounds apiece.

In these first six stories, Conan Doyle established the pattern that would characterize virtually all future Sherlock Holmes stories (and their many imitations). Often they begin with a brief scene unrelated to the main story, in which Holmes's powers are demonstrated, or they may start with references to other cases Holmes has solved, which are given tantalizing names ("the giant rat of Sumatra," "the arrest of Wilson, the notorious canary-trainer") but not described. The mystery is then introduced by the entrance of a distressed client with a story to tell, or one of the several Scotland Yard detectives who sneer at Holmes but still turn to him when they are stumped. The problem is laid out in detail, with Holmes seizing on what seem to the others in the room to be trivial or even foolish details. The mysteries are told from the point of view of Dr. Watson, who admires Holmes, but is frequently bewildered by him.

Because Holmes generally declines to explain his motives, the reader is left, like Watson, to watch as Holmes goes about his investigation and try to figure out what on earth he is doing. In the end, Holmes, who has a strong dramatic streak, produces his solution with a theatrical flourish. Once everyone has admitted to being baffled by his apparently miraculous knowledge, he explains, in the manner of Dr. Joseph Bell, exactly how he created the chain of reasoning that led him to the answer, following his maxim "Once you have eliminated the impossible, whatever remains, *however improbable, must be the truth.*" And, as Holmes sometimes complains, once he has laid everything out clearly, the conclusion is so obvious that people tend to decide he has not really been so clever after all.

The Strand Magazine commissioned Sidney Paget to do the illustrations for the first Holmes stories,

"'I SUPPOSE THAT YOU ARE THE DETECTIVES FROM LONDON?' SAID HE."

In this scene from "The Adventure of the Dancing Men," illustrator Sidney Paget shows Holmes wearing the deerstalker cap that would become one of his most recognizable attributes.

but they had made a mistake—they had really meant to ask his brother Walter, also an illustrator. Although Walter Paget thus missed out on his chance to illustrate Sherlock Holmes, Holmes nonetheless made him immortal, for Sidney used Walter as a model. His drawings created the very definite idea of Sherlock Holmes's appearance that readers still have today, and every illustrator or actor who has portrayed him since has made him look something like Walter Paget. Conan Doyle always generously claimed that Sidney Paget had helped create Sherlock Holmes. In a toast at a banquet, he said, "Sidney Paget . . . illustrated these stories so well that he made a type which the whole English-reading race came to recognise." It was Paget, who wore such a costume himself, who first showed Holmes in the deerstalker cap and Inverness cape that are today universally associated with him. However, he depicts Holmes wearing these only in the country, never in the city, where they would not have been considered appropriate. In London,

73

Holmes dressed like a proper Victorian gentleman.

The Sherlock Holmes stories began to appear in *The Strand Magazine* in July 1891 and were an explosive success. At the beginning of every month, people eager to see the newest Sherlock Holmes story as soon as it left the press formed long lines at the magazine office and at booksellers' stalls. London libraries stayed open late the night a new story came out. Almost immediately, people began to act as if Sherlock Holmes really existed. Conan Doyle began to receive letters addressed to Holmes or Watson, asking for advice, offering services, expressing admiration, and sending gifts of tobacco and violin strings. Letters addressed simply to "Sherlock Holmes, London," reached Conan Doyle with no trouble.

Conan Doyle always credited Dr. Joseph Bell with being the inspiration for Holmes. In gratitude, he stood a photograph of Bell prominently on his mantelpiece, and he wrote to Bell, "It is most certainly to you that I owe Sherlock Holmes. . . . I do not think that his analytical work is in the least an exaggeration of some effects which I have seen you produce in the out-patient ward." *The Strand* published an article by Bell in which he compared the work of a detective to that of a medical diagnostician and praised the Sherlock Holmes stories highly. Bell even sent Conan Doyle some ideas for further Sherlock Holmes stories, although none of them worked out.

Bell realized that, although Conan Doyle had borrowed one of his distinctive features for the detective, Sherlock Holmes was a very different character from Joseph Bell. "Dr. Conan Doyle's genius and intense imagination has on this slender basis made his detective stories a distinctly new departure," he wrote to one journal, "but he owes much less than he thinks to yours truly, Joseph Bell." Like Conan Doyle, Bell began to receive letters from people who saw him as a real-life Holmes and asked him for help in solving mysteries. This diminished his enthusiasm, and, impatient of all the unwanted attention, he became almost as tired of Sherlock Holmes as his creator would soon be. In a letter to a friend he complained, "Why bother yourself about the cataract of drivel for which Conan Doyle is responsible? I am sure he never imagined that such a heap of rubbish would fall on my devoted head in consequence of his stories."

The success of the Sherlock Holmes stories finally convinced Conan Doyle that he was a writer, not a doctor who wrote on the side. After almost dying from a severe attack of influenza, he took a serious look at his life and decided to give up his medical practice. "I determined with a wild rush of joy to cut the painter and to trust for ever to my power of writing," he recalled. In June 1891, only a few months after he had come to the city, he moved with his wife, daughter, sisters, and mother-in-law into a large house with a garden in South Norwood, on the outskirts of London. (His mother, who valued her independence, declined to join the household.) Life at Norwood was pleasant and happy. Conan Doyle's first son was born in 1892, and named Alleyne (after the young hero of *The White Company*) Kingsley.

As the publication of the last of the Holmes stories that *The Strand Magazine* had on hand approached, and the public's enthusiasm continued to grow, the magazine asked Conan Doyle for six more. He, however, had already moved on to something else. He was planning to write a historical novel set in the 17th-century French court and in North America, and he wanted to spend his time researching the Iroquois Indians and the Canadian wilderness. To get the *The Strand* to leave him alone, he decided to quote them such a high price for six Holmes stories that they would not want to pay it. "The Strand are simply imploring me to continue Holmes," he wrote to his mother. "I will write by this post to say that if they offer me £50 each, *irrespective of length,* I may be induced to consider my refusal. Seems rather high-handed, does it not?" But *The Strand* agreed immediately.

The second set of six stories included "The Adventure of the Speckled Band," often considered to be the best of all the Holmes mysteries. In this story, a terrified young woman consults Holmes because she hears a mysterious whistling in the night—just as her sister had heard in the nights before she died crying out, "Oh my God. . . . It was the band. The speckled band." As he worked on these

In this letter, Conan Doyle told his mother he is thinking of "slaying Holmes" in the last story of the group he was working on. She persuaded him to let Holmes live, at least for the time being. In place of the story he had planned, he took his mother's "golden haired idea" mentioned in the letter and adapted it to become "The Adventure of the Copper Beeches."

> Tennyson Road.
> Nov 11 /91.
>
> Dearest Mam -
>
> I have done five of the Sherlock Holmes stories of the new series. They are 1. The Adventure of the Blue Carbuncle 2. The Adventure of the Speckled Band 3. The Adventure of the Noble Bachelor 4 The Adventure of the Engineer's Thumb 5. The Adventure of the Beryl Coronet. I think that they are up to the standard of the first series, & the twelve ought to make a rather good book of the sort. I think of slaying Holmes in the sixth & winding him up for good & all. He takes my mind from better things. I think your golden haired idea has the making of a tale in it, but I think it would be better not as a detective tale, but as a separate one.

stories, Conan Doyle decided that it really was time to be done with the detective. There was only one thing that would definitely bring the series to an end. "I think of slaying Holmes in the last and winding him up for good. He takes my mind from better things," he wrote to his mother. The Ma'am, who was one of Sherlock Holmes's greatest fans, wrote back, "You won't! You can't! You *mustn't!*" And he didn't. She even offered him an alternate plot to replace the death of Holmes, which became "The Adventure of the Copper Beeches." In this story, a woman hired as a governess because of her distinctive hair color appeals to Holmes because she fears that her employer is using her for some sinister purpose.

He began serious work on his American book, *The Refugees,* but *The Strand* was writing to him again. "They have been bothering me for more Sherlock Holmes tales," he wrote to his mother. "Under pressure I offered to do a dozen for a thousand pounds, but I sincerely hope they won't accept it now." This payment, if he received it, would make him the highest-paid short-story writer ever up to that time. Somewhat to his surprise, *The Strand* agreed. He had several other projects on hand by now, including a Napoleonic novel and a play, so he asked for more time to write—he would squeeze in a moment for Sherlock Holmes when he could. Privately, he determined that this time he would kill off his creation no matter what his mother said.

In the meantime, he and his wife went on a Continental tour. In Switzerland, with Sherlock Holmes still preying on his mind, he visited the village of Meiringen and "I saw there the wonderful falls of Reichenbach, a terrible place and one that I thought would make a worthy tomb for poor Sherlock, even if I buried my bank account along with him." He kept his resolve. In April 1893, he wrote to his mother, "I am in the middle of the last Holmes story, after which the gentleman vanishes, never to return. I am weary of his name." In his diary he noted laconically, "Killed Holmes." The last of the new dozen stories he sent *The Strand* was "The Final Problem," in which Sherlock Holmes falls to his death in the Reichenbach Falls, taking with him his dire enemy Professor James Moriarty, "the Napoleon of Crime." The story ends with Watson grieving for "the best and the wisest man whom I have ever known."

The death of Sherlock Holmes caused a sensation among his readers. On the streets of London, men wore black crepe armbands and hatbands in mourning. Conan Doyle was deluged with furious letters, including his favorite, from a woman who began, "You brute!" Perhaps most upset of anyone was *The Strand,* which had lost one of its most valuable properties. The magazine's circulation dropped by 20,000. At the end of "The Final Problem," *The Strand* printed a notice untruthfully and somewhat desperately assuring its readers, "There will be only a temporary interval in the Sherlock Holmes stories. A new series will commence in an early number." In the meantime, the magazine began to print imitations by other writers, but none developed the following of Holmes.

Arthur Conan Doyle seemed to be the only man in England who was not sorry Sherlock Holmes was dead. In *Memories and Adventures* he recalled, "The general protest against my summary execution of Holmes taught me how many and how numerous were his friends. I heard of many who wept. I fear I was utterly callous myself." Conan Doyle has become known as "the man who hated Sherlock Holmes" (to quote the title of one biography), and it is true that he frequently spoke of Holmes as a burden he wished he could get rid of. His chief complaint was that the popularity of the Holmes stories prevented people from adequately appreciating his other works. "All things find their level," he wrote in his autobiography, "but I believe that if I had never touched Holmes, who tended to obscure my higher work, my position in literature would at the present moment be a more commanding one."

Conan Doyle never truly realized the value of the stories he wrote so easily. He was a man of his time, and the Victorian middle class tended to distrust anything that was too much fun, valuing high moral seriousness and hard work over humor or pleasure. However, although he always stated his case against Sherlock Holmes in these moralistic terms, his real complaint seems to have had more to do with the enormous demands the character's popularity made on him. Holmes gave him no rest. He wrote the stories as fast as he could, and before he had even finished one batch, everyone was demanding more. He had wide-ranging interests and wanted to try many different kinds of stories, but whenever he turned to any other area of writing, someone was sure to ask him for more Holmes. As he explained to a reporter from the *Cincinnati Commercial Gazette* who reproached him for killing Holmes, "Ah, but I did it in self-defense. And if you knew the provocation you would agree that it was justifiable homicide. . . . No sooner had one story appeared than I was set upon for another. . . . At last I killed him, and if I had not done so I almost think he would have killed me."

Perhaps Conan Doyle's attitude toward his creation is revealed most clearly in a letter in which he told a friend, "Poor Holmes is dead and damned. . . . I have had such an overdose of him that I feel towards him as I do towards *pâte-de-foie-gras,* of which I once ate too much, so that the name of it gives me a sickly feeling to this day."

From "The Final Problem"

When Conan Doyle wrote this passage, he genuinely believed that he was giving Sherlock Holmes's last words, and he allowed his creation to go out with considerable stoicism and nobility, sacrificing himself to the greater good. Having allowed Watson to be called away on what he knew to be a false errand, Holmes awaits Professor Moriarty and almost certain death alone at the Reichenbach Falls in Switzerland. Although Moriarty is an archvillain, responsible for most of the crime in England, Holmes nonetheless shows perfect confidence in his honor as a gentleman: If Moriarty has given his word, it would be unthinkable for him to take unfair advantage by attacking before Holmes finishes writing his farewell to Watson.

But it was destined that I should, after all, have a last word of greeting from my friend and comrade. It consisted of three pages torn from his notebook and addressed to me. It was characteristic of the man that the direction was as precise, and the writing as firm and clear, as though it had been written in his study.

A few words may suffice to tell the little that remains. An examination by experts leaves little doubt that a personal contest between the two men ended, as it could hardly fail to end in such a situation, in their reeling over, locked in each other's arms. Any attempt at recovering the bodies was absolutely hopeless, and there, deep down in that dreadful cauldron of swirling water and seething foam, will lie for all time the most dangerous criminal and the foremost champion of the law of their generation. . . . As to the gang, it will be within the memory of the public how completely the evidence which Holmes had accumulated exposed their organization, and how heavily the hand of the dead man weighed upon them. Of their terrible chief few details came out during the proceedings, and if I have now been compelled to make a clear statement of his career, it is due to those injudicious champions who have endeavoured to clear his memory by attacks upon him whom I shall ever regard as the best and the wisest man whom I have ever known.

MY DEAR WATSON [it said]:

I write these few lines through the courtesy of Mr. Moriarty, who awaits my convenience for the final discussion of those questions which lie between us. He has been giving me a sketch of the methods by which he avoided the English police and kept himself informed of our movements. They certainly confirm the very high opinion which I had formed of his abilities. I am pleased to think that I shall be able to free society from any further effects of his presence, though I fear that it is at a cost which will give pain to my friends, and especially, my dear Watson, to you. I have already explained to you, however, that my career had in any case reached its crisis, and that no possible conclusion to it could be more congenial to me than this. Indeed, if I may make a full confession to you, I was quite convinced that the letter from Meiringen was a hoax, and I allowed you to depart on that errand under the persuasion that some development of this sort would follow. Tell Inspector Patterson that the papers which he needs to convict the gang are in pigeonhole M, done up in a blue envelope and inscribed "Moriarty." I made every disposition of my property before leaving England and handed it to my brother Mycroft. Pray give my greetings to Mrs. Watson, and believe me to be, my dear fellow,

Very sincerely yours,
SHERLOCK HOLMES

8

CONAN DOYLE, SPORTSMAN

Conan Doyle was not in England to be witness to the public's grief over Sherlock Holmes's death, and he would have been in no mood to sympathize with it in any case, for he was dealing with tragedies of his own. In October 1893, his father died. Shortly after, he began to suspect that his wife Touie, who had been sick ever since their return from Switzerland, was suffering from more than a passing illness. An examination confirmed that she had tuberculosis (or consumption, as it was called at the time), and the doctors gave her only a few months to live. There was still no known cure for tuberculosis—Conan Doyle had confirmed this himself on his trip to Germany three years earlier—but like a true knight he was determined to battle for his wife's life as long as possible. "We must take what Fate sends," he wrote to his mother, "but I have hopes that all may yet be well." The only response to tuberculosis that was known to make any difference was moving to a more healthful climate. Conan Doyle was not happy at the idea of spending the forseeable future in resorts abroad, but his chivalrous nature made it natural for him to devote himself to Touie. (In her usual gentle and self-effacing way, she left the deci-

Conan Doyle in 1894 experimenting with a pair of "Norwegian skis," which he introduced to Switzerland. Conan Doyle, who had a horror of sounding conceited, liked to caricature himself as a comic bungler—and in this case his depiction seems not wholly inaccurate.

sion entirely up to him.) Leaving the children with their grandmother, he gave up the home in Norwood and moved with Touie to a hotel in Davos, Switzerland.

Touie's health began to improve immediately, and Conan Doyle plunged into life in Switzerland with his characteristic zest. Several years earlier, on a trip to Norway, he had seen skis used, and he had recently been reading about their use for traveling in Greenland. Finding that they were virtually unknown in Switzerland, he wrote away for a few pairs. Before the amused eyes of the villagers and hotel residents, he taught himself to use them, with frequent undignified falls that led him to remark, "On any man suffering from too much dignity, a course of skis would have a fine moral effect." He then enlisted the help of two local sportsmen, the Branger brothers, and they set off to discover what could be done with these skis.

The three men set out to ski to the town of Arosa, in the next valley. During the winter, Arosa could be reached from Davos only by taking a long railroad trip around the mountain, but Conan Doyle and his friends managed to ski over the high pass—although they almost killed themselves in the process and Conan Doyle tore a large hole in the seat of his pants. At the hotel in Arosa, Tobias Branger registered Conan Doyle as "Conan Doyle, Sportesmann," which he valued as much as any compliment he ever received. "You don't appreciate it as yet," Conan Doyle had told the hotel guests at Davos, "but the time will come when hundreds of Englishmen will come to Switzerland for a skiing season." In his autobiography, he notes, "I think I am right in saying that these and other excursions of ours first demonstrated their possibilities to the people of the country. . . . If my rather rambling career in sport has been of any practical value to any one, it is probably in this matter."

By October 1894, Touie's health was so much better that Conan Doyle decided he could accept an invitation from the entrepreneur Major J. B. Pond to go on a lecture tour of the United States. He had felt a particular interest in the United States ever since reading Edgar Allan Poe and Bret Harte as a child. His second published story was called "The American's Tale," and many of his stories were set in the United States, including half of *A Study in Scarlet*. At a time when most Englishmen thought of Americans as money-grubbing, tobacco-spitting boors, Conan Doyle believed that Americans and Englishmen were natural allies, and advocated a close relationship between the two countries. "I have always longed to see America, and I have always longed also to see a warmer friendship between the two great nations of the English-speaking race," he wrote to a friend.

Conan Doyle was not particularly interested in talking about himself; he proposed to deliver two lectures that had been popular in England: "George Meredith and His Work," and "The Younger Influences in English Literature." He was persuaded to add a third lecture that was more personal and included readings from his own works, although, as he wrote to a friend, "This last I included under protest, owing to strong representations from Pond, my agent." The agent was right—the third lecture was by far the most popular. Audiences came to hear Conan Doyle because they loved his stories, especially those about Sherlock Holmes. In fact, some came hoping to actually see Holmes. According to a New York newspaper, when Conan Doyle appeared, broad-shouldered, hearty, and smiling genially, "a thrill of disappointment ran through the assembly," who had been hoping for someone cold, gaunt, and intense.

If any Americans really were disappointed at first that Conan Doyle did not look like Sherlock Holmes, they certainly got over their disappointment quickly. He made a strongly favorable impression wherever he went. Over and over again he is described in the same terms. According to the *New York Times,* "He is tall, straight, athletic, and his head that his blue eyes make radiant with affability must have been modeled by Energy herself, so profoundly impressed it is with her mark." The *New York Recorder* added, "There are few physical gifts that are so delightful as a hearty, cheery, sympathetic voice, and such a voice is one of Dr. Doyle's most charming powers." The *Ladies' Home Journal* reported, "His personality is a peculiarly attractive one to Americans, because it is so thoroughly wholesome. The first impression which he makes is one of entire health of body and mind. . . . Simple, sincere, unaffected and honest, Dr. Doyle has that background of old English qualities which united with great kindliness of spirit and courtesy of manner, makes friends and holds them."

Because he wanted to return to Touie in time for Christmas, he crowded a lot into a small space of time. "I have lectured at New York, Chicago, Milwaukee, Cincinnati, Indianapolis, Detroit, Toledo, Boston, Worcester, etc. etc. etc.," he wrote to a friend, and he often lectured more than once in a day. Pond filled every spare minute with social engagements. Conan Doyle found the whole schedule exhausting. Particularly difficult for him was meeting admirers after the lectures, and he always tried to dodge them. Despite the bluff and hearty impression he gave, he still felt the same nervous shyness that had set him trembling when he had spoken to the Portsmouth Literary Society so many years before. On one occasion, when Pond told him that he was to meet a group of prominent New York ladies after his lecture, he replied, "Oh Major, I cannot, I cannot. What do they want of me? Let me get away. I haven't the courage to look anybody in the face."

From everyone's point of view, the American trip was a success. Pond paid Conan Doyle a businessman's greatest compliment, saying, "I would give him more money to-day than any Englishman I know of if he would return for a hundred nights." Even U.S. newspapers approved of this rare Englishman who actually spoke well of the United States, and they returned the favor. "He was one of the most

Conan Doyle, who enjoyed physical activity of all kinds, with his bicycle. In the early days of their marriage, he and Touie rode a tandem tricycle.

appreciative Englishmen that ever came to this country," remembered Pond. "He was a great favourite with the newspaper men, and they were always ready and willing to say nice things of him." His friendly relations with the American press would later stand him in good stead.

Returning to Davos, Conan Doyle found his wife's health still improving. While in the United States, he had read audiences his first story featuring a new character—Brigadier Gerard, a hotheaded, vain, and brave soldier serving under Napoleon—with whom he hoped to repeat the kind of success he had with Sherlock Holmes. Americans had loved the comical brigadier, and Conan Doyle spent the winter writing more stories about him. When these stories were eventually published in *The Strand,* they proved

Conan Doyle visited Egypt several times. Although his second wife, Jean, is riding a camel, he seems to have retained his early mistrust of this animal and is riding a donkey instead.

immensely popular, but the character never attained the legendary status of Holmes. Conan Doyle spent his free time that summer laying out a golf course for himself, an activity that was hampered by the tendency of passing cows to chew up his flags.

In the fall of 1895, he returned to England to settle some business. Here he met a friend who told him that his own consumption had been cured by the air of Hindhead, Surrey, in southern England. "It was quite a new idea to me that we might actually live with impunity in England once more," he wrote, "and it was a pleasant thought after resigning oneself to a life which was unnatural to both of us at foreign health resorts." He immediately bought a plot of land and commissioned a friend of his from Southsea to design and build him a house.

While they waited for the house to be finished, Conan Doyle decided to take Touie to Egypt, where he hoped the hot, dry climate would complete her cure. Here, too, Conan Doyle discovered, Sherlock Holmes had established himself. Translated into Arabic, the stories were being used by the police as a textbook. For six months, the Conan Doyles lived in a hotel near Cairo, where Touie continued to recover, and Conan Doyle enjoyed himself in his usual vigorous fashion. He had brought with him an entire reference library so that he could continue with the Brigadier Gerard stories, but he found it hard to concentrate on his work. He climbed the Great Pyramid "once, and was certainly never tempted to do so again," and decided to learn horseback riding.

When Touie was strong enough, the Conan Doyles took a tour up the Nile River to the Sudan. Although the cruise passed without event, this area was dangerously unstable. The Sudan was ruled jointly by Egypt and England, but since 1881, followers of a Muslim movement called the Mahdists had been fighting to retake it. Conan Doyle was fascinated by a visit to a little mud village that had just been raided by Mahdist Dervishes on camels. "The survivors seem quiet and cheerful enough," he recorded in his diary, "but 17 of them were killed by their assailants." Tours traveled to the Sudan on a regular schedule, and were not particularly well protected. Conan Doyle did not see what was to prevent the Dervishes from sweeping down on one of the tours. "If I were a Dervish general," he wrote, "I would undertake to carry off a Cook's excursion party with the greatest ease." His next novel, *The Tragedy of the Korosko,* tells the story of just such an event.

Although no English tourists were ever actually carried off, the British government decided it was time for the British Empire to step in and restore order. In 1896, just before the Conan Doyles were scheduled to leave Egypt, Major General Horatio Kitchener, the commander of the army, received orders to retake the Sudan. Conan Doyle was excited. He had always longed to see battle, and now he had his chance. "It is impossible to be near great historical events and not to desire to take part in them, or at least to observe them," he remarked in his autobiography. "Clearly I could not remain in Cairo, but must get up by hook or by crook to the frontier." Eagerly he offered to act as an unpaid war correspondent for the *Westminster Gazette,* so that he would be allowed to visit the front lines.

With four reporters and a guide, he crossed the desert by camel. This was a dangerous journey during which the small, unprotected group risked attack by Dervishes, but all Conan Doyle actually encountered was a poisonous adder in his bed and a large scurrying creature that he took to be a mouse but turned out to be a tarantula. He seems to have felt that the real danger was his camel. "Its appearance is so staid and respectable that you cannot give it credit for the black villainy that lurks within," he wrote. "It approaches you with a mildly interested and superior expression, like a Patrician lady in a Sunday school. . . . It puts its lips gently forward, with a far-away look in its eyes, and you have just time to say, 'the pretty dear is going to kiss me,' when two rows of frightful green teeth clash in front of you. . . . When once the veil is dropped, anything more demoniacal than the face of a camel cannot be conceived."

They reached the front only to discover that the British army would not be able to attack for several weeks. First it needed to find several thousand camels. Conan Doyle could not wait that long; it was almost summer, when the heat would be bad for Touie, and he had to take her back to England. He missed the decisive battle, which did not take place until September 2, when the British—using machine guns—would kill 11,000 Mahdist fighters while losing only 48 of their own men. Not experiencing the battle was a bitter disappointment, but Conan Doyle found one silver lining—he donated his camel to the British Empire and traveled back by cargo boat.

It was not Conan Doyle but actor William Gillette, in his stage adaptation of the Sherlock Holmes stories, who put into Holmes's mouth the immortal words "Elementary my dear Watson."

9

"I RATHER FELT IT WAS MY DUTY"

Back in England, the Conan Doyles settled into a quietly happy life at their new home, "Undershaw," in 1897. Now, for the first time, Conan Doyle found himself considering a return to Sherlock Holmes. He started a play featuring the detective, but was unable to complete it satisfactorily. The great actor-manager Beerbohm Tree expressed interest, but he wanted the character of Holmes revised to suit his own acting style better. Despite repeated claims that he did not care about Holmes, Conan Doyle was unwilling to distort the character. "Rather than re-write it on lines which would make a different Holmes from my Holmes, I would without the slightest pang put it back in the drawer," he decided.

However, he did not care what other people did. A few years later, when the American actor William Gillette asked for permission to rewrite the play, he consented. Gillette, not sure how far he was allowed to go with revisions, sent a cable asking: MAY I MARRY HOLMES? Conan Doyle replied: YOU MAY MARRY HIM OR MURDER HIM OR DO ANYTHING YOU LIKE WITH HIM. And so Holmes first appeared on stage in the United States, with enormous success, and ended the

Jean Leckie, who would become Conan Doyle's second wife, was utterly devoted to him. "In all the twenty-three years we were married, I never heard an ignoble or unkind word pass his lips. His soul and mind were incapable of it," she wrote in a memoir.

play engaged to be married. It was Gillette who introduced the curved-stem pipe with which Holmes is today frequently shown—supposedly Gillette found that an ordinary pipe hid his face and muffled his lines.

On May 15, 1897, Conan Doyle's own married life suddenly became much more complicated. At the age of 38, he fell passionately in love with a beautiful young woman named Jean Leckie, and she with him. Jean, whom he probably met at a party, was a much more dashing and energetic figure than Touie. The daughter of a wealthy Scottish family, she rode horses, hunted, and had trained as a singer in Europe. Conan Doyle was determined to deal with the situation like a perfect gentleman. The idea of having an affair was absolutely foreign to him. He resolved that nothing should induce him to hurt Touie, who was not strong and these days rarely left home. He told Jean he thought the situation was unfair to her and gave her the opportunity to break off their friendship, but she refused. And so he assumed the attitude of a knight in a chivalric romance toward his ideal lady—she was his to serve and worship from afar, and his conduct would be a test of his nobility. The relationship would remain purely spiritual. It is a sign of his sincerity that his mother became a confidante for both Jean and Conan Doyle. "It is sweet to think of Jean with your sweet motherly arms round her," he wrote to his mother gratefully. "Was there ever such a love story since the world began? How many folk in the world have ever had their love tested as ours has been?"

From the outside it is hard not to see the pair as, in some sense, waiting for Touie to die so they could get married, but they never consciously allowed themselves to consider such a thought. Conan Doyle continued to devote himself to his wife. "I have nothing but affection and respect for Touie," he told his mother. "I have never in my whole married life had one cross word with her, nor will I ever cause her any pain." He loved her for her gentleness and self-sacrifice, but his feelings for Jean were a passion he had not felt before. "Touie . . . is as dear to me as ever," he explained to his brother Innes, "but . . . there is a large side of my life which was unoccupied but is no longer so." Doctors had predicted that Touie would be dead three years earlier. In fact, she still had 10 years to live. During all this time Conan Doyle's relationship with Jean remained absolutely platonic, and as far as anyone knows, Touie never learned about Jean.

Maintaining both relationships and his sense of honor was a great strain on Conan Doyle. "My soul is naturally and inevitably rather wrenched in two all the time," he told his mother. Perhaps partly to keep his mind occupied, Conan Doyle stayed very busy. He wrote several novels, including *A Duet,* his portrait of a marriage, and started *Sir Nigel,* the companion book to *The White Company.* He adapted a short story about the reminiscences of an old British soldier, the last survivor of a regiment that helped conquer Napolean, into his one-man play, *Waterloo,* which he sent to Henry Irving, the greatest actor of the day, who fell in love with it and purchased it on the spot. When the play opened in Bristol (after some delay), there was so much excitement about it that a special train was chartered, filled with all the critics who wanted to go see it. Conan Doyle also traveled and lectured frequently, and involved himself in public affairs. In particular, he interested himself in the army, writing suggestions to the war office, which they ignored.

In 1899, the Boer War broke out in South Africa. This was a conflict between Great Britain and the Dutch settlers—the Boers—chiefly over who would have control of the area's rich mining and farming resources. (Native South Africans remained largely uninvolved in the conflict, and their claims were ignored by both sides.) Conan Doyle immediately and eagerly volunteered. Despite her enthusiasm for chivalry, his mother was not pleased. "My own dearest and very naughty son," she wrote. "How dare you, what do you mean by it? Why, your very height and breadth would make you a simple and sure target, and is not your life, to say the least, of more value, even to your country—at home? Think of the pleasure and solace your writings afford to thousands. . . . There are hundreds of thousands who can fight for *one* who can make a Sherlock Holmes or a Waterloo!"

His response shows clearly the way Conan Doyle saw his position in the world, and how seriously he took it. "I was afraid that you would be angry with me for volunteering. But I rather felt it was my duty. . . . What I feel is that I have perhaps the strongest influence over young men, especially young athletic sporting men, of any one in England, (bar Kipling)." Less idealistically, he also admitted, "It would bore me to remain in England."

The Ma'am need not have worried. He was now 40 years old, and the army did not want him. Soon after he was rejected, he received an offer—"in a capacity which was less sporting but probably . . . a good deal more useful," as he wrote in his memoirs—to go as the supervisor of a private, civilian-run field hospital being set up. He had some doubts. The senior doctor was a gynecologist, "a branch of the profession for which there seemed to be no immediate demand," as he commented. The military officer attached to the hospital drank too much. And Conan Doyle's own medical experience was now long behind him. Still, this was his best chance to get involved in the war, so he agreed, working for free and paying all his own expenses.

The hospital was set up in tents on a cricket ground at Bloemfontein. At one end stood some discarded sets for a production of the operetta *H.M.S. Pinafore,* which were used as latrines. Shortly after Conan Doyle's team arrived, the Boers captured the nearby waterworks, and with no sanitary water available, a virulent enteric (typhoid) fever broke out. In a space intended for 50 patients, there were soon 120 dead and dying men, crowded into any available spot on the floor. Conan Doyle, an early believer in the controversial theory of inoculation, had been voluntarily inoculated for enteric fever on the way over, and he did not catch the disease. However, 12 of 15 staff members became ill, and the remaining few were frantically overworked.

In *Memories and Adventures,* Conan Doyle graphically recalls the terrible conditions: "We lived in the midst of death—and death in its vilest, filthiest form. . . . The nature of the disease causes constant pollution . . . of the most dangerous character and with the vilest effluvia. . . . A haze of flies spreads over everything, covering your food and trying to force themselves into your mouth—every one of them a focus of disease." An average of 60 people a day died in the small town and were buried in shallow mass graves. The stench of death could be smelled from as far as six miles away.

After four weeks the waterworks were recaptured, the fever subsided, and the army moved on. For the first time, Conan Doyle was able to take a few days off. All his life, he had wanted to witness a battle firsthand. As soon as he arrived in South Africa, he had walked seven miles out and seven miles back in an unsuccessful attempt to see one. Now, he set off to the front to see some real action. Despite the horrors he saw, he found "something of exhilaration in the feeling" of being in battle, as he wrote in his account of

Arthur Conan Doyle stands in a trench during the Boer War in South Africa, where he served as the supervisor of a field hospital.

his experiences. Conan Doyle saw war as a great game, played honorably, with respect for the rules and for the enemy as long as they fought like gentlemen. This was a common view, in a time when army commissions were still purchased by upper-class families for their sons, and it would have been shared by most of his readers. Even in the midst of battle, after having fought death heroically for weeks, he embraced the game with gusto. In his moment-by-moment description of battle, shells flying, "Wheeeeee—ooof," and "Boom! Boom! Boom! Cannon at last!" and the men joking, and shouting challenges and insults at the enemy, he is clearly enjoying himself very much. "When the millennium [which would bring an end to all war] comes," he wrote, "the world will gain much, but it will lose its greatest thrill."

All the time he was in South Africa, he had been collecting firsthand descriptions from soldiers and generals, hoping to write the definitive history of the Boer War. When the British captured Pretoria, in June 1900, it seemed the war was practically over, and Conan Doyle returned home. "What adventures I have had too!" he told his mother. "I have . . . seen many wondrous things."

But shortly after he returned to England, the war entered a new stage of guerrilla warfare, which lasted several more years. Conan Doyle corresponded with as many generals and soldiers as he could, to ensure that his coverage of this phase of the war would be as immediate as his dicussion of the first. *The Great Boer War,* published in 1900, was very successful, and was praised for both its accuracy and its fairness. The final chapter contained Conan Doyle's recommendations for modernizing the British army. Most of his ideas—which included relegating swords to the museums in favor of rifles, and reorganizing the army democratically, by merit instead of social class—were ignored at the time, but by the end of World War I they had all been adopted.

In 1900, soon after his return from South Africa, Conan Doyle was asked to stand for a seat in Parliament, representing the Unionist party (named for its support of a union between Ireland and Great Britain). Always eager for a good fight, he decided to run in his old hometown of Edinburgh, which was a stronghold of the opposition. He was considered to have no chance of winning, but with his forceful personality and the moving sincerity of his speeches, he began to gain support. Of course he insisted on a clean and honorable fight. "We have a letter which would damn our opponent utterly but I won't let them use it," he confided to his mother. "It is below the belt."

Until the day of the election, it looked as if he might actually win. That morning, however, someone pasted signs all over town accusing him of being part of a Catholic plan to dominate England. There was no time to respond to this preposterous accusation, and because anti-Catholic feeling was strong, it was enough to make him lose the election, although by only 600 votes. Thus, Conan Doyle managed to fulfill the family tradition of suffering for the Catholic faith, even though he had long ago dropped it. In 1906, he was persuaded to try standing for Parliament again, but his heart was not in it, and when he was again defeated, he decided to abandon organized politics.

What Conan Doyle called "one of the most pleasing and complete episodes of my life" involved his second book on the Boer War. This war had been controversial even in Great Britain—Conan Doyle's own mother believed the Boers were in the right—and Great Britain had been widely criticized abroad. The Boers accused the British of atrocious conduct—rape, torture, establishing concentration camps, and destroying farms. Germany was particularly vocal in criticizing British conduct. The British government made no attempt to counter these accusations, believing that its conduct spoke for itself and any official defense would be demeaning. Conan Doyle, who had seen the British army in action and was confident of its essential honor, was enraged at the criticisms. He still believed a European war was probable in the near future, and he considered it important that Great Britain should not be alienated from its friends. He was especially suspicious of Germany's sudden humanitarian pose and believed (correctly, as it turned out) that it was encouraging the rumors in order to weaken Great Britain's position. He found himself wondering why no one was writing a response, and then "like a bullet through my head, came the thought, 'Why don't you draw it up yourself?'"

He immediately plunged into the task. He had been present during the worst of the war, had spoken to many of the soldiers involved, and already had specific, firsthand evidence he could use to demonstrate that, although the war had certainly been brutal and destructive, the British had not been the ruthless villains they were being painted as. Conan Doyle planned to write a pamphlet that would be translated into many languages and be widely distributed in

From "His Last Bow"

In "His Last Bow," one of the few Sherlock Holmes stories written in the third person, Holmes poses as an informer betraying the British government. He has shown his usual shrewd good sense by making sure he receives payment for his faked information before capturing the dangerous German spy he has been pursuing, and then revealing himself. Like Conan Doyle, Holmes senses the approach of World War I, although Watson, as usual, is several steps behind him, and takes Holmes's thoughtful prediction literally.

"As to you, Watson, you are joining us with your old service, as I understand, so London won't be out of your way. Stand with me here upon the terrace, for it may be the last quiet talk that we shall ever have."

The two friends chatted in intimate converse for a few minutes, recalling once again the days of the past, while their prisoner vainly wriggled to undo the bonds that held him. As they turned to the car Holmes pointed back to the moonlit sea and shook a thoughtful head.

"There's an east wind coming, Watson."

"I think not, Holmes. It is very warm."

"Good old Watson! You are the one fixed point in a changing age. There's an east wind coming all the same, such a wind as never blew on England yet. It will be cold and bitter, Watson and a good many of us may wither before its blast. But it's God's own wind none the less, and a cleaner, better, stronger land will lie in the sunshine when the storm has cleared. Start her up, Watson, for it's time that we were on our way. I have a check for five hundred pounds which should be cashed early, for the drawer is quite capable of stopping it if he can."

Great Britain and abroad, all paid for by public subscription. An appeal to his publisher and the war office, and to the public through a letter in the *Times,* brought him almost immediately all the money and facilities that he needed. It almost seemed as though all Great Britain had been waiting for him to ask. He also received many donations from Englishmen living abroad who were upset at how they were being perceived, and 500 pounds from "a Loyal Briton" who was almost certainly King Edward VII.

The Cause and Conduct of the War in South Africa was written in one intensive effort over the course of nine days in January 1902. The "pamphlet," as Conan Doyle referred to it, although it was some 60,000 words in length, was remarkable for its fairness. He did not ignore cases where British conduct might be open to criticism but attempted to state both sides completely and backed up all his assertions with evidence. "I kept my individual opinions in the background, and made a more effective case by marshalling the statement of eye-witnesses, many of them Boers, on the various questions of farm-burnings, outrages, concentration camps, and other contentious subjects. I made the comments as simple and short as I could." In fact, much of the text consists of direct quotations from civilians and military men, including French and Austrians, as well as Boers.

In Great Britain the book, which cost sixpence, quickly sold 300,000 copies. Translations were distributed abroad to journalists, clergymen, and other community leaders at no cost. Among the French, Dutch, Welsh, Hungarian, Norwegian, Swedish, Portuguese, Spanish, Italian, and Russian editions, more than 141,000 copies were issued. Because his book was not special pleading but was so clearly a sincere attempt to get at the facts, it seems to have been genuinely effective in turning the tide of public opinion. It was widely read and discussed and, "there was a rapid and marked change in the tone of the whole Continental press, which," as Conan Doyle remarks with characteristic modesty, "may have been a coincidence but was certainly a pleasing one."

Sales were so successful that some money was left over when the project was completed. This money was used to establish a scholarship to educate a South African student in England. The intent was to bring over one of their former opponents, that is, someone of Boer descent. However, the first winner of the scholarship was a scholar, who, as Conan Doyle recalled in his autobiography, pointed out that "there could be no question as to his eligibility, as he was a full-blooded Zulu."

For his service to the nation, Conan Doyle was offered a knighthood. His first inclination was to refuse it. "It is a silently understood thing in the world that the big men . . . do not condescend to such things," he wrote to his mother, with his unique mixture of vanity, humility, and idealism. "Not that *I* am a big man, but something inside me revolts at the thought. . . . All my work for the State would seem tainted if I took a so called 'reward.' It may be pride and it may be foolish, but I could not do it." He called knighthood "the badge of the provincial mayor." To the Ma'am, however-er, knighthood was still the glorious honor of chivalry, and she could not bear the thought of his refusing it. She pointed out also that refusal might seem an insult to the king. He gave in, although not happily, and on August 9, 1902, he became Sir Arthur Conan Doyle. Many years later, in his story "The Three Garridebs," Conan Doyle would take the chance to show the public what he thought about it by informing them that, in 1902, Sherlock Holmes had been offered a knighthood and had refused it.

Arthur Conan Doyle was knighted in 1902. "They have also made me Deputy-Lieutenant of Surrey, whatever that means," he wrote to his brother Innes. This photograph shows him in his Deputy Lieuten-ant's uniform, which he complained made him look like a monkey on a stick.

THE RETURN OF SHERLOCK HOLMES

Arthur Conan Doyle received his knighthood because of his service to his country in the Boer War, but few people remember this fact, and some refused to believe it even at the time. For that same year, he had done something else that in the public eye made him worthy of any honor. He had brought back Sherlock Holmes.

Holmes was still dead—Conan Doyle insisted on that—but in *The Hound of the Baskervilles* he allowed Watson to tell one of their earlier adventures. The idea for this book came in 1901, when his friend Fletcher Robinson told him some legends of the bleak northern region of England called Dartmoor, renowned chiefly for its maximum security prison. Conan Doyle's imagination was fired in particular by the story of a ghostly supernatural hound that had haunted one family for generations, and he decided to use it as the basis of a novel. He found the legend so great an inspiration that he spoke of Robinson as coauthor of the book, even though he had almost certainly written none of it. Together the two men explored the bleak moors, prehistoric stone huts, and prison of Dartmoor, gathering material for what, he wrote to his

Basil Rathbone (right), one of the best film actors to play Sherlock Holmes, in The Hound of the Baskervilles, *with Nigel Bruce as Watson.*

mother, would be "a real Creeper."

He did not originally conceive of the book with Holmes in mind, but as he started work, he realized that he would need a strong, intelligent central character around whom he could organize it. "So I thought to myself," he explained to a friend, "why should I invent such a character when I had him already in the form of Holmes?" Conan Doyle had been indifferent to pleas and even threats from readers and publishers who wanted him to revive Holmes, but now he himself chose to do so. The result pleased everyone. In Conan Doyle's own opinion, "Holmes is at his very best, and it is a highly dramatic idea." The reading public showed its approval by sending the circulation of *The Strand Magazine* up 30,000 copies in August 1901 when the serial began to appear.

In an interview shortly afterward, Conan Doyle gave the first hint that news of Sherlock Holmes's death might have been exaggerated. "I know that my friend Dr. Watson is a most trustworthy man, and I gave the utmost credit to his story of the dreadful affair in Switzerland," he told *Harper's Weekly*. "He may have been mistaken, of course." Then, finally, in the September 1903 edition, *The Strand* was able to announce to its readers that a new series of Sherlock Holmes stories would begin appearing in its next issue.

Conan Doyle had been away from the character long enough not to shrink from him. In the spring of 1903, when an American publisher made the princely offer of $5,000 per story for the U.S. rights alone if he would find some way to bring Sherlock Holmes back to life, he was ready to accept. He replied tersely to his agent, "Very well. A. C. D." This sounds less than enthusiastic, but when his mother suggested that perhaps trying to revive a former success was risky, he defended the idea vigorously: "I am not conscious of any failing powers," he replied. "I have not done any Holmes short-stories for seven or eight years"— actually it was closer to ten—"and I don't see why I should not have another go at them."

The actual device to explain away Holmes's death was suggested to him by Jean Leckie. Holmes had not been killed when he fell off the cliff, Watson explained, because he had never actually fallen. When Conan Doyle killed off Holmes in "The Final Problem," he certainly intended that death to be final. But perhaps, unconsciously, he had wanted to keep the option of reviving him someday, because he left himself several obvious loopholes that now made the task much easier. No one had witnessed Holmes's death, and his body had never been recovered, or, as Conan Doyle himself wrote, "fortunately no coroner had pronounced upon the remains, and so, after a long interval, it was not difficult for me to respond to the flattering demand and to explain my rash act away. I have never regretted it."

He brought Holmes back to life very ingeniously. "The Adventure of the Empty House" reveals that the detective had practiced "baritsu, or the Japanese system of wrestling" (which does not actually exist), to save himself from falling off the cliff. For the past three years he had been traveling as "a Norwegian named Sigerson" to various exotic and inaccessible places, concealing his survival so that he could entrap the remaining members of Professor James Moriarty's gang. He returns to London, and to life, to spring the trap he has set to catch Colonel Sebastian Moran, who has taken Moriarty's place as "the most cunning and dangerous criminal in London."

Conan Doyle was pleased with his new Sherlock Holmes stories. He told his mother that "The Adventure of the Empty House" was "a rare good one," and of the first four stories, "I have got three bull's-eyes and an outer." (The last was "The Adventure of the Solitary Cyclist," which he never liked much.) Despite his frequent complaints that the Sherlock Holmes stories obscured his more important work, he made it clear in his autobiography that he did not consider the new ones hack work. "I was determined, now that I had no longer the excuse of absolute pecuniary pressure, never again to write anything which was not as good as I could possibly make it, and therefore I would not write a Holmes story without a worthy plot and without a problem which interested my own mind. . . . If the public find, as they will find, that the last story is as good as the first, it is entirely due to the fact that I never, or hardly ever, forced a story." Nonetheless, and despite the overwhelming enthusiasm the public showed, he could not help worrying. "The writing is easy. It is the plots which butcher me," he confided to his mother. "Will they take to Holmes?"

Of course they took to Holmes, as enthusiastically as they always had. Conan Doyle never again attempted to kill Holmes off. He reappeared periodically for the rest of Conan Doyle's life, although (with one exception) the stories do not move into the present, but continue to be set in turn-of-the-century England. In fact, Holmes reappeared so many times that in the introduction to *The Case-book of Sherlock Holmes,* the very last collection of stories, Conan Doyle wrote, "I fear that Mr. Sherlock Holmes may become like one of those popular tenors who, having outlived their time, are still tempted to make repeated farewell bows to their indulgent audiences. This must cease and he must go the way of all flesh, material or imaginary." The last Sherlock Holmes story, "The Adventure of Shoscombe Old Place," appeared in 1927, only three years before Conan Doyle's death.

Readers have been debating the relative merits of the stories from before and after Holmes's "death" ever since they appeared. The new stories did have some plot holes, but then, so had the old ones. Conan Doyle always insisted that the new Holmes stories were every bit as good as the first set, and suggested reading the series in reverse to prove it. However, he quoted with amusement the Cornish boat-man who said to him, "I think, sir, when Holmes fell over that cliff, he may not have killed himself, but all the same he was never quite the same man afterwards."

Sherlock Holmes's supposed death had occured just as Touie's illness was discovered. Now, shortly after he came back to life, she was dying. After living 13 years longer than doctors had predicted, Louise Conan Doyle died in July 1906. Despite Conan Doyle's love for Jean Leckie, Touie had been his constant companion, and the ideal Victorian wife—generous, self-effacing, and unquestioningly supportive—for 21 years. Conan Doyle took her death very hard. In his private diary he wrote, "Standing by her body I felt that I had done my best." Still, it is hard to imagine he did not feel some guilt as well for his long involvement with Jean.

For the first time in his life, he suffered from ill health, boredom, and depression, and could not work. Characteristically, he fought his way out of this darkness by focusing on someone else's distress, fighting passionately against what he believed was a miscarriage of justice. Conan Doyle had frequently been asked to investigate real mysteries, but, although he occasionally offered suggestions, he had usually been wary of doing so, claiming that he was not particularly observant. In December 1906, he read an appeal from a young man, George Edalji, for help in clearing his name. "As I read, the unmistakable accent of truth fixed itself upon my attention and I realised that I was in the presence of an appalling tragedy and that I was called upon to do what I could to set it right," he recalled.

George Edalji was the son of a rural clergyman in the small village of Great Wyrley. Reverend Edalji was an Indian of Parsee descent, and therefore, in British eyes, a "black." The Edaljis were used to a certain amount of hostility from narrow-minded people who resented a black of "heathen" ancestry presuming to be the spiritual adviser and social equal of white Englishmen, but they had experienced no real trouble until 1888, when they began receiving a series

Conan Doyle commented that George Edalji's protruding eyes alone were enough indication that his eyesight was too poor for him to commit the crimes he had been convicted of.

of vicious anonymous letters. The police concluded, against all evidence, that George Edalji was the culprit. The chief constable, George Anson, demonstrated his closed mind by informing the parents in regard to one accusation, "I may say at once that I shall not pretend to believe any protestations of ignorance which your son may make." For seven years the letters had stopped; then they had resumed, more malicious than ever. More distressingly, farm animals were being slashed at night and left to bleed to death, and the anonymous letters threatened that soon the same thing would start happening to the village girls.

The police immediately arrested George Edalji, who by now had a promising career as a solicitor (a member of the legal profession who advises clients and represents them in the lower courts and who prepares cases for barristers to try in the higher courts). The inspector confiscated Edalji's overcoat, which he stored with a piece of horsehide cut from one of the animals that had been slashed—then later used the fact that there were horsehairs on this coat as evidence. When Edalji turned out to have an alibi for the times the slashings apparently occurred, the prosecution, as Conan Doyle put it, "shifted its ground," deciding that the incidents must have happened some other time so that Edalji could have done them. While Edalji was in jail awaiting trial, another horse was mutilated.

Because the case against him seemed too ludicrous to be considered a threat, the defense did not bother going into detailed arguments. But Edalji was convicted and sentenced to seven years in prison at hard labor. Protests and a petition with 10,000 signatures had succeeded in getting Edalji released from jail after three years, but he was still considered guilty, and he had lost the right to work as a solicitor.

The wrongs done to George Edalji, Conan Doyle wrote, "would have been almost comic had they not had so tragic an upshot." It did not require Sherlock Holmes's penetrating intelligence to realize that Edalji was the victim of racial prejudice. Moreover, when Conan Doyle met with him, as a former eye doctor he realized at once that Edalji was almost blind. He could not possibly have made his way through fields and a tunnel after dark, climbing over wires and crossing a railroad track while evading patrolling police officers, as the prosecution's story required.

Conan Doyle wrote a series of articles for the *Daily Telegraph,* laying out in his clear, reasonable, and unbiased style all the facts of the case. He did not actually say much that had not already been said in Edalji's defense—but he was Arthur Conan Doyle, the creator of Sherlock Holmes, and he was willing to let Holmes's name be used in a good cause. SHERLOCK HOLMES IS HAVING ONE MORE "LAST ADVENTURE" AND THIS TIME IN REAL LIFE announced the *Daily Telegraph* headline. His articles created such a storm of protest that the Home Office was forced to reconsider the charges. England had at that time no procedure established for a retrial, so instead a private committee met. It declared Edalji innocent of the mutilations, but decided he was responsible for the anonymous letters. "Assuming him to be an innocent man," the report said, "he has to some extent brought his troubles on himself." Years later this decision still enraged Conan Doyle. "It was a wretched decision," he wrote, "and the Law Society . . . showed what they thought of it by at once readmitting Edalji to the roll of solicitors with leave to practise. . . . It is a blot upon the record of English Justice." The *Daily Telegraph* raised money to pay for Edalji's defense, but he received no compensation for his three years in jail.

Conan Doyle was not satisfied. He set out to discover who had written the letters. "All my energies have gone towards the capture and exposure of the real offenders," he wrote to his mother. He began to receive vicious anonymous letters himself. "Desperate men have sworn their Bible oath to scoop out your liver and kidneys," he was warned. He came up with a suspect, and his evidence was certainly more compelling than that against Edalji, but the police refused to consider it, and Edalji was never completely cleared. Partly as a result of this scandal, a Court of Criminal Appeal was finally established in England later in 1907.

In recent years, some new facts have been brought to light about the Edalji case. Conan Doyle could never understand why the police were so sure George had written the anonymous letters, with no evidence at all. In fact, they had been given a vicious letter that had supposedly been taken from George's drawer. Their informant was George's older brother Horace, who was estranged from the family. Because the prosecution never mentioned this evidence, it was unavailable for the defense to address. It has been speculated that Horace Edalji (who later changed his name) might have had some connection with the letters, and decided to incriminate his brother to divert suspicion from himself. George Edalji moved to London after his partial vindication in 1907 and died in 1953, at the age of 85. The anonymous letters and cattle slashings continued until 1915, long after he had moved away.

Conan Doyle's generous exertions on the Edalji case helped him through the year he waited before he felt ready to marry Jean Leckie. In September 1907, when they were finally married, George Edalji was a guest at the wedding reception. "There was no guest whom I was prouder to see," said Conan Doyle. Edalji gave the couple the works of Tennyson and Shakespeare as a wedding gift.

"Having just got clear of the Edalji case," Conan Doyle wrote in *Memories and Adventures,* "I became entangled in that of Oscar Slater. Since I was generally given credit for having got Edalji out of his troubles, it was hoped by those who believed that Slater's condemnation was a miscarriage of justice that I might be able to do the same for him." It is not clear exactly who approached Conan Doyle about Slater or when, but after the frustration of his partial victory for Edalji, Conan Doyle was very reluctant to become involved in another case. Moreover, although Conan Doyle considered Edalji to be an exemplary young man, he did not approve of Slater, whom he called "a not very desirable member of society." A German Jew, Slater was a gambler and pawnbroker, and lived with a mistress. Despite his distaste, Conan Doyle said, "When I glanced at the facts, I saw that it was an even worse case than the Edalji one, and that this unhappy man had in all probability no more to do with the murder for which he had been condemned than I had." Conan Doyle was wise enough to realize that his prejudices were irrelevant to the case.

The Slater case is a very tangled one. Briefly, the facts are these. In 1908, in Scotland, Marion Gilchrist, a well-off, elderly lady living alone except for a servant girl, was brutally murdered while the servant, Helen Lambie, was out of the house for a moment. When a neighbor and Lambie went into the house together, they passed a man whom Lambie seemed to recognize. Gilchrist's papers had been searched, but the only thing that seemed to be missing was a diamond brooch.

When Oscar Slater shortly thereafter attempted to pawn a diamond brooch, police assumed they had their suspect. Slater's brooch was not the one that had been taken from Gilchrist, however, and he was able to prove he had owned it for years.

Oscar Slater in 1928, the year after he was finally released from prison, having served more than 17 years. He died in 1949.

Nonetheless, although this piece of jewelry was the only link the police had to Slater, they decided he was guilty. By displaying a photograph and asking leading questions, they got Lambie and another girl, who had happened to be in the street, to identify Slater as a man seen in the area. Later the two again identified him—after he was pointed out to them. Gilchrist had been murdered with a heavy instrument that might have been a hammer, and the police were able to prove the damning fact that Slater (in common with perhaps half the population of Scotland) actually owned a hammer. Slater had an alibi; he was home with his mistress—but because she was not a lawful wife, her evidence was not admitted.

The evidence against Slater was so ridiculous that he could not believe he would be convicted—but he was. Slater was condemned to hang, but the sentence was commuted to imprisonment for life after a petition from 20,000 concerned citizens called for his pardon. "It is an atrocious story," wrote Conan Doyle, "and as I read it and realized the wickedness of it all, I was moved to do all I could for the man."

Once again Conan Doyle wrote up the case and succeeded in getting the conviction reconsidered. However, the rehearing was held privately, the witnesses were not under oath, and important new evidence from a police detective who was able to show that Helen Lambie had originally named another man, until convinced by the police to identify Slater, was ignored. Conan Doyle was enraged, but felt he could do no more.

Years later, in 1925, a released prisoner smuggled out a message from Slater by hiding it under his tongue. In it Slater implored Conan Doyle to take up the case again. The authorities turned down requests for another rehearing. A journalist, William Park, who was interested in the case, had uncovered more evidence of police misconduct and suppression of evidence that had led to the conviction, and Conan Doyle himself published the book Park wrote, adding a preface. Both witnesses who had identified Slater came forward and withdrew their identifications, adding that their statements had been dictated by the police. Slater was released, and was paid 6,000 pounds in compensation for his eighteen and a half years of wrongful imprisonment.

"Sir Conan Doyle, you breaker of my shackels, you lover of truth for justice sake, I thank you from the bottom of my heart," Slater wrote. Yet the story was not quite over. Many people, including Conan Doyle, had advanced money to pay for Slater's expenses, and Conan Doyle felt that Slater was honor-bound to use his compensation to pay them back. Slater refused, and Conan Doyle wrote to him, "You are the most ungrateful as well as the most foolish person whom I have ever known."

There were many other, smaller cases in which Conan Doyle used Sherlock Holmes's methods to help someone. Years later one of his sons, who always claimed that Conan Doyle had based Holmes on himself, wrote, "My memories as a youth are mottled with sudden, silent periods when, following upon some agitated stranger or missive, my father would disappear into his study for two or three days on end." In his autobiography, Conan Doyle lists with satisfaction cases when he was able to find a missing person or save a woman from a deceiver, but he also recalls the time when the police had already found and arrested the culprit "while I had got no farther than that he was a left-handed man with nails in his boots."

The frontispiece of Three of Them, *Conan Doyle's book about his three children by his second wife, Jean. "Billie" is his daughter Jean, "Dimples" is Adrian, and "Laddie" is Denis.*

11

"A GRAND CHANCE OF A WONDERFUL EXPERIENCE"

The years before World War I were busy and happy ones for Sir Arthur Conan Doyle. He was finally married to Jean, for whom he had waited so long. Of their idyllic union he wrote after 17 years, "There are some things which one feels too intimately to be able to express, and I can only say that the years have passed without one shadow coming to mar even for a moment the sunshine of my Indian summer." They moved to a house called Windlesham in Sussex to be near Jean's family. Kingsley and Mary, now in their teens, were fortunately very fond of Jean, and Touie, on her death bed, had told Mary that she should not be upset if her father remarried. The couple had three children, Denis, Adrian, and Jean, and Conan Doyle wrote a book about their antics, called *Three of Them,* published in 1923.

By now, Arthur Conan Doyle had established himself as one of the most prominent figures of his time. He remained eager to use his power to fight for the weak and helpless against injustice. In 1909, he was approached by a man named Roger Morel, who asked if he would use his influence to press for reform in the Belgian Congo. Conan

Doyle had no particular previous knowledge of the issues, but as he read the evidence collected by Morel and British consul Roger Casement, it aroused all his chivalrous instincts. When Europe had colonized Africa, the Congo had become, as the so-called Congo Free State, in effect the private preserve of King Leopold II of Belgium. Most of the land was jungle, and very little accurate information about conditions there reached the outside world. Leopold ruled the land with a vicious cruelty that was horrifying even by the standard of the general European exploitation of Africa. Natives were not allowed to work their own lands, but could only serve the state, which set them arbitrary and impossible rubber production quotas. Starvation and disease, murder, torture, and grotesque mutilations were the daily tools of the government.

Once he had satisfied himself that the evidence was valid, Conan Doyle went to work with his usual energy, writing the 45,000-word *Crime of the Congo* in eight days, lecturing throughout England, and writing to influential figures such as United States President Theodore Roosevelt, Kaiser Wilhelm II of Germany, and Winston Churchill (then a rising British politician) to enlist their support. In a letter sent to 60 U.S. newspapers, he summarized his position: "Never before has there been such a mixture of wholesale expropriation and wholesale massacre, all done under the odious guise of philanthropy." When criticized for the violence of his language, he replied, "sometimes violence is a duty." Reform finally came to the Congo under Leopold's successor. Morel's tribute to Conan Doyle vividly demonstrates the real power that Conan Doyle's reputation and personality had earned him: "Conan Doyle's intervention at that time exercised a decisive influence on the course of events. . . . Yet it was not his book—excellent as it was, nor his manly eloquence . . . which helped us most. It was just the fact that he was—Conan Doyle."

Conan Doyle continued to involve himself in any issue

where he felt he could be of use. When Roger Casement was later convicted of treason springing from his fierce devotion to Irish independence, which had led him to collaborate with Germany, Conan Doyle headed the movement to spare him from the death penalty. He argued that Casement was "a fine man afflicted with mania," and that his homosexuality, which had weighed heavily against him, was irrelevant. Conan Doyle campaigned for reforms in the divorce laws that would make them less biased against the woman. He did not support votes for women, however, on the grounds that, "When a man comes home from his day's work, I don't think he wants a politician sitting opposite him at the fireside." (He would, however, make an exception for those few women who paid taxes.) The suffragettes several times poured corrosive acid in his mailbox.

One of the uses Conan Doyle made of the power his fame gave him was to serve as an unofficial goodwill ambassador for Great Britain. When a group of French officers visited Great Britain in 1905, in an official effort to promote friendship between two nations traditionally suspicious of each other, he was delighted that they asked to visit the author of Sherlock Holmes. In the United States, he was referred to by the former U.S. ambassador to Great Britain as "the best known living Britisher." He was invited by the editor of the *New York Morning Telegraph,* who knew of Conan Doyle's love of boxing and his reputation for fairness, to act as referee in the championship boxing match in which for the first time a black man was challenging a white man, "because of [the] extremely friendly feeling for you in America." He wanted very much to go, but could not spare the time from his Belgian Congo campaign. (Jack Johnson, the black champion, won, defeating Jim Jeffries.) In 1914, he was invited to tour the Canadian west in his own railway car, as a guest of the Canadian government. On this, his second visit to North America, he discovered baseball and was asked to open a baseball game. No one

Conan Doyle standing next to his car, a 20-horsepower Dietrich-Lorraine, during Prince Henry's International Road Competition. Jean rode with him, and the German officer assigned to accompany them endeared himself to Conan Doyle by putting fresh flowers in her corner of the car every day.

expected he would actually hit the ball the first time he ever held a baseball bat, but, drawing on his cricket skills, he hit a hard line drive and almost flattened a photographer.

From one effort at building international understanding, Conan Doyle recalled in *Memories and Adventures,* he "came away . . . with sinister forebodings"—his participation in the International Road Competition organized by Prince Henry of Prussia in 1911. This was not a race, but a challenge designed to test the quality of the automobiles produced by the two different countries. A group of British cars and a group of German cars followed a winding route from Hamburg, Germany, to London, traveling about 150 miles a day. Each car carried an officer from the opposite team, who would deduct points for any mechanical problems. From the start, there was hostility in the air. Although Conan Doyle, one of the few British competitors who spoke German, did his best to bring about a more cordial atmosphere, and tried scrupulously to be fair, he came away with little respect for the honor of the Germans. "Personally the competitors were not a bad set of fellows, though there were some bounders among them," was the best he could say about them. Afterward he concluded, "There can be no doubt in looking back that a political purpose underlay it. The idea was to create a false entente." He also suspected (rightly) that the Germans were using the competition as an excuse to survey the English countryside for military purposes. Almost everyone involved came away convinced that war was coming. At least the British won the road competition.

Despite an active public life that would have exhausted most men, Conan Doyle also continued to write prolifically. In addition to several historical novels and another series of Sherlock Holmes stories, written mostly to please Jean, in 1910 he indulged his love of boxing and his fascination with the theater by writing and producing a play. *The House of Temperley* was loosely based on his 1896 novel *Rodney Stone,* which dealt with professional boxing during the English Regency period. Critics had been skeptical about boxing as an appropriate subject for a book, and they were equally skeptical about the play. So he rented a theater for six months and paid for the production himself.

At first the play was surprisingly successful, especially the realistically staged fight scenes, but interest soon faded, and the death of King Edward VII, which led to a brief moratorium on theatergoing, finished the play off. Conan Doyle was left with the rent for an expensive theater. He could have sublet it, but instead he turned to his old friend Sherlock Holmes. Within a month he had written, staged, and opened *The Speckled Band,* featuring Sherlock Holmes and Doctor Watson. The play, which earned Conan Doyle back much more than he had lost, was wildly successful, especially after a real snake—which refused to act—was replaced by a lively mechanical one.

Conan Doyle created one final series character, based

on another of his former Edinburgh professors, William Rutherford. In his billiard room, Conan Doyle kept a set of fossilized footprints he had found on the Sussex downs outside his house. Described by him as "huge lizard tracks," they had been made by an iguanodon, a kind of dinosaur. Fascinated by the idea of a prehistoric monster in his own backyard, he began to read about dinosaurs, and decided to write a book about them.

The Lost World tells the story of an expedition to a remote and virtually inaccessible plateau in the largely unexplored South American jungle where, isolated from the rest of the world, dinosaurs still survive. Leading the expedition is Professor George Edward Challenger, a monstrously vain, hot-tempered, and very funny character who, with his aggressive, overwhelming personality, recalled Professor Rutherford, with a touch of Dr. George Budd. In 1911,

A scene from the movie of The Lost World. *When Conan Doyle showed excerpts from this movie to the annual meeting of the Society of American Magicians, he managed, without actually lying, to convince them they were seeing psychic photography of something real.*

dinosaurs were not nearly as popular or well known as they are today, and Conan Doyle had to explain them to his readers. "I think it will make the very best serial (bar special S. Holmes values) that I have ever done," he told his editor at *The Strand Magazine*. "My ambition is to do for the boy's book what Sherlock Holmes did for the detective tale. I don't suppose I could bring off two such coups. And yet I hope it may."

Professor Challenger does not share Sherlock Holmes's popularity today, but in a sense Conan Doyle accomplished what he hoped to. *The Lost World* can be considered the ancestor of all the dinosaur stories that have followed. Challenger proved popular enough to be featured in three more science fiction novels. In *The Poison Belt,* Challenger and his friends wait in a sealed room as the earth passes through a band of poisonous gas that he has predicted will kill the entire human race. Despite its somber theme, the novel contains some very funny scenes, most notably one in which Challenger, under the influence of the gas, hides under the table and bites his housekeeper's leg. *When the World Screamed* tells the story of Challenger's attempt to prove that the earth is a living creature, by drilling a hole deep into its core. The minor novel *The Disintegration Machine* is about a machine that can dissolve and remake matter, including people.

As with previous stories, Conan Doyle wanted to give *The Lost World* circumstantial trappings that would create the illusion of its being real: "faked photos, maps, and plans." He sat for a photograph in which he, as Professor Challenger, appeared in a heavy black beard, eyebrows, and a wig. When *The Strand* declined to use the photograph, fearing that they would be accused of a hoax, he decided the disguise was too good to waste. So he visited his brother-in-law Willie Hornung, Connie's husband, in the character of a professor from Germany, and managed to fool him for a few minutes before being indignantly thrown out.

FROM *THE LOST WORLD*

Very little was known about dinosaurs when Conan Doyle wrote The Lost World *in 1911, and he was able to give his imagination free reign. As he imagines them, pterodactyls sound like rather unpleasant potential pets; nonetheless, the explorers bring one back with them and release it before an amazed crowd in London to prove the truth of their story.*

The place into which we gazed was a pit, and may, in the early days, have been one of the smaller volcanic blow-holes of the plateau. It was bowl-shaped, and at the bottom, some hundred yards from where we lay, were pools of green-scummed, stagnant water, fringed with bulrushes. It was a weird place in itself, but its occupants made it seem like a scene from the Seven Circles of Dante. The place was a rookery of pterodactyls. There were hundreds of them congregated within view. All the bottom area round the water-edge was alive with their young ones, and with hideous mothers brooding upon their leathery, yellowish eggs. From this crawling flapping mass of obscene reptilian life came the shocking clamour which filled the air and the mephitic, horrible, musty odour which turned us sick. But above, perched each upon its own stone, tall, grey, and withered, more like dead and dried specimens than actual living creatures, sat the horrible males, absolutely motionless save for the rolling of their red eyes or an occasional snap of their rat-trap beaks as a dragon-fly went past them. Their huge, membranous wings were closed by folding their forearms, so that they sat like gigantic old women, wrapped in hideous web-coloured shawls, and with their ferocious heads protruding above them. Large and small, not less than a thousand of these filthy creatures lay in the hollow before us.

Even without the faked photographs, *The Lost World* may have managed to fool someone. According to a 1913 press release, "A few days ago the yacht *Delaware* left Philadelphia. . . . The yacht is the property of the University of Pennsylvania, and is bound for Brazil . . . in the interest of science and humanity. They seek Conan Doyle's 'lost world,' or some scientific evidence of it." Conan Doyle doubted these explorers had seriously believed his Lost World existed, especially because the date of the press release was April 1, but he said they were bound to find something interesting, even if it was not dinosaurs.

A few years later, Conan Doyle created the illusion that his dinosaurs were real even more dramatically. In 1922, he was invited to the annual meeting of the Society of American Magicians. At the end of the meeting, he mounted the stage to perform his own trick. The next day's *New York Times* headlines describe what happened next: DINOSAURS CAVORT IN FILM FOR DOYLE. SPIRITIST MYSTIFIES WORLD-FAMED MAGICIANS WITH PICTURES OF PREHISTORIC BEASTS—KEEPS ORIGIN A SECRET. Because Conan Doyle was known to believe in "spirit photography," which claimed to be able to capture on film things not normally visible, the reporter suggested that perhaps Conan Doyle was "lifting the veil" and had managed to photograph dinosaurs from the past, using spiritual powers. The "monsters of the ancient world, or of the new world, which he has discovered in the ether, were extraordinarily life-like," he wrote. "If fakes, they were masterpieces." After the article appeared, Conan Doyle revealed that what he had actually shown were scenes from a movie in progress of *The Lost World,* created by the early special effects wizard Willis O'Brien, who was later responsible for fabricating the first King Kong in the 1933 movie about the giant ape.

As it grew clear to him that World War I was inevitable, Conan Doyle turned his talent for deceptively realistic fiction to the service of his country. He had long believed that the British government underestimated the danger posed by the new kind of naval vessel with which Germany was experimenting—U-boats, or submarines. He advocated the building of a tunnel between France and England, to ensure that England could not be cut off from Europe. To his frustration, he could not convince anyone to listen. He wrote a story called "Danger!" in which a small country with no military resources except a fleet of submarines declares war on England and actually wins. He wanted *The Strand Magazine* to send his story to leading admirals and publish their comments along with the story.

He had a very convincing bribe for them, too. *The Strand* agreed to publish "Danger!" in the manner he wished, and in their edition of August 14, 1914, they were also able to announce: CONAN DOYLE'S GREAT NEW SERIAL "THE VALLEY OF FEAR" THRILLING WITH INCIDENT AND EXCITEMENT WILL COMMENCE IN OUR NEXT NUMBER. Conan Doyle had given them his final Sherlock Holmes novel, a mystery based on the vicious struggle between unions and mine owners in the United States.

"Danger!" attracted some interest, but made few converts. Of the admirals who gave *The Strand* their responses, only one agreed with Conan Doyle's assessment of the potential danger posed by submarines. Most responses reflected the old attitude of war as a gentleman's game— submarines just were not very sporting, and they could trust that the enemy's sense of "fair play" would prevent their use. The idea of building a tunnel between England and France was raised in Parliament, but nothing came of it. The channel tunnel (or "chunnel") was not built until 1994. Later Conan Doyle's predictions were proved to be absolutely correct. As a naval secretary in the German Reichstag remarked in 1916, "The German people can thank the British Admiralty for disregarding the warning on U-boat warfare given by Sir Arthur Conan Doyle." "I wish my argument had proved less sound," Conan Doyle wrote in his memoirs.

When World War I broke out in 1914, Conan Doyle turned his multiple talents to the service of his country. He attempted to enlist, but he was 55 years old—well over age. He then founded a Civilian Reserve Corps, in which he was very happy practicing drills, and encouraged the growth of a network of similar corps around the country. Although he was ordered by the War Office to stop this unofficial military action, he was appointed to the government committee that established the official reserve corps, and his own group became the first unit. "I found the life of a private soldier a delightful one," he wrote, nicknaming himself "Ole Bill." He was particularly pleased by a pompous adjutant who called him, "my man," assuming he was an ordinary private, and was then horrified to be told by the commanding officer, "That's Sherlock Holmes."

Conan Doyle bombarded the war office with ideas and suggestions, most of which were ignored. He did, however, convince the government to supply sailors on warships with rubber vests, and later rubber life rafts, an innovation that saved many lives, because these devices did not burn when the boat was torpedoed. "I need hardly say that I never received a word of acknowledgment or thanks from the Admiralty," he complained. "But it may be that some poor seaman struggling in the water sent me his good wish, and those are the thanks that I desired." He was also a determined advocate of protective metal helmets on the battlefield, which the army eventually adopted.

Having been asked by the government to write some morale-building articles, he was allowed to visit the English, French, and Italian fronts, and he used his wide acquaintance to convince numerous officers and soldiers to send him firsthand accounts of the fighting. While the war was still in progress, he was already at work on what would become the six-volume *History of the Great War,* explaining it battle by battle, with great clarity and balance. By the time the war was over, however, few people wanted to relive it in such detail, and there was little interest in the work. He referred to this as "the greatest and most undeserved literary disappointment of my life."

Conan Doyle's World War I writings reveal his somewhat ambivalent attitude toward war. In a fit of passion unusual for him, he wrote, "May God's curse rest upon the arrogant men and the unholy ambition which let loose this horror upon humanity!" But it is also clear in his accounts of his visits to the front that he was having a wonderful time. In a letter to Innes, he described the possibility of being part of the fighting as a "grand chance of a wonderful experience." And he called the war "the physical climax of my life as it must be of every living man and woman." All his life, Conan Doyle seems to have felt most alive in exciting, immediate physical situations, even if they involved deadly risk—he has been described by Sherlock Holmes scholar Michael Harrison as an "adrenaline addict."

Sherlock Holmes also played his part in the war. After an encounter with the French General Georges Humbert, who ("to my horror," wrote Conan Doyle) asked him if Sherlock Holmes was serving in the British army, he wrote the only Holmes story that brings the detective into the modern age. In "His Last Bow," Watson uses a telephone and drives a car as he helps Holmes capture and defeat a German spy. Conan Doyle also put his real-life detective skills to use to secretly get accurate information to British prisoners being held at Magdeburg. He sent a copy of one of his books to a friend who was captured there. Starting in the third chapter (because he believed the guards would check early pages more carefully) he marked letters with a pinprick to inscribe secret messages. In the accompanying letter he advised the recipient "that the book was, I feared, rather slow in the opening, but that from Chapter III onwards he might find it more interesting."

World War I robbed Conan Doyle of many of the

important people in his life. Malcolm Leckie, Jean's favorite brother, was the first to be killed. Conan Doyle also lost two nephews and his brother-in-law Willie Hornung, a close friend. His beloved brother Innes and his only son with Touie, Kingsley, survived the fighting, but, weakened by injuries, they both died in the flu epidemic that followed the war.

A "spirit photograph" of Arthur Conan Doyle taken in 1919. The ghostly head is supposedly his son Kingsley, who had died the year before. Photography was in its early stages, and people could be fooled with fairly crude fakes, since it was generally thought that photographs did not lie.

12

"HOMO SAPIENS! HOMO IDIOTICUS!"

During World War I, Sir Arthur Conan Doyle experienced what, for him, was the most important moment of his life, but it had nothing to do with deaths or battles. Since his days in Southsea, he had been cautiously interested in spiritualism. In late 1915, something convinced him that its claims were completely true, and he became a devout spiritualist. After years of study and investigation, he wrote, "I felt at last no doubt at all." No one knows exactly what this decisive event was, but it probably involved a message from beyond the grave, perhaps from Jean's brother Malcolm Leckie, who had just been killed at the front.

It has often been said that Conan Doyle's conversion to spiritualism was caused by his many losses during the war. In fact, his conversion happened before the most painful losses—the deaths of his son and brother. Still, it certainly did bring him consolation when they died, and when his beloved mother died a few years later. "It is," he wrote, "a revolution in religious thought . . . which gives us an immense consolation when those who are dear to us pass behind the veil."

Conan Doyle now viewed his whole rich and varied life as nothing but a prelude to his real existence. He had discovered his true purpose—to spread the gospel of spiritualism. "The rest of my life," he wrote a friend, "will be spent in endeavoring to show the human race how blind and deaf they have been in not understanding the great new spiritual forces which have come in so strange a fashion into the world." He spent the last 15 years of his life preaching spiritualism.

Belief in spirits is at least as old as recorded history, but the spiritualism that bloomed in the years after the Great War was a particular religion serving the needs of a society that had seen an entire generation die in battle. The fundamental tenets of this movement are that the soul survives death with its personality intact; that the living can contact the souls of the dead; and that these things are not a matter of faith, but can be proved scientifically. The central act of the spiritualist movement was the seance. At this gathering, a specially gifted person called a "medium" would go into a trance and the spirits would speak through him (or more usually, her). To prove their existence, they would play tambourines, knock on tables, or give other physical signs of their presence. They might write long messages through the medium, and they could be photographed. They took form using a strange substance called "ectoplasm" drawn from living people. Usually a medium had a "spirit guide"—a specific spirit who helped channel and control the spirits. The guide at Conan Doyle's family seances was an Indian named Pheneas who wrote (through Conan Doyle) a book called *Pheneas Speaks*.

It is easy now to laugh at the spiritualists, but most people in the early 20th century had lived through such extraordinary and world-altering discoveries as evolution, the use of electricity, sound recording, automobiles, and airplanes—they had seen powerful new forces discovered and harnessed, and were open to the possibility that more such transformative agents might exist. "We have seen of late years, in such matters as wireless or heavier-than-air machines that the most unlikely things may come to pass," Conan Doyle advised readers. "It is most dangerous to say a priori that a thing is impossible."

For Conan Doyle, an important aspect of spiritualism was that it presented itself as a science, not a religion. All his life he had mistrusted faith as a dangerously irrational form of belief that leads to intolerance and strife. Spiritualism did not demand faith; instead it offered the skeptic objective proof. Because of his medical training, Conan Doyle considered himself a scientist, and he always stressed the fact that he had spent his entire adult life evaluating the proofs offered for spiritualism, and had not been easily convinced.

As early as his medical school days, he had attended a lecture on the survival of the spirit after death and decided it was "a clever thing indeed. Though not convincing to me." Over the years, as he personally experienced more and more phenomena that he could not explain away, he had tried to maintain an open mind. He was swayed by the writings of people he knew as reputable scientists. Sir William Crookes, the chemist and physicist noted for his work on radioactivity, and Alfred Russel Wallace, who independently formulated the theory of evolution at about the same time as Darwin, were the most prominent scientific supporters of spiritualism. "I, too, have studied Spiritualism for many years, and cannot easily dismiss it, in spite of the presence of frauds," he wrote to a friend. "It is hard to put aside the experiences of trained observers like Crookes, Russel Wallace, etc., and say that it was a delusion. I believe that there was objective truth in their observations." He frequently used this appeal to scientific authority. "Either the observers are liars or lunatics—or their observations are true," he wrote to the *Sunday Express,* adding that "among these observers are many of the first scientific brains in the world."

text continues on page 136

FROM *THE LAND OF MIST*

In his final Professor Challenger book, the earnestness of Conan Doyle's desire to deliver his spiritualist message often gets in the way of the story. By the end of the book, the truth of spiritualism has been proven to the satisfaction of Challenger, the quintessential scientist. He becomes a much tamer character, but the obstreperous warrior of the previous books has not completely vanished.

Challenger had himself altered. His colleagues, and those about him, observed the change without clearly perceiving the cause. He was a gentler, humbler, and more spiritual man. Deep in his soul was the conviction that he, the champion of scientific method and of truth, had, in fact, for many years been unscientific in his methods, and a formidable obstruction to the advance of the human soul through the jungle of the unknown. It was this self-condemnation which had wrought the change in his character. Also, with characteristic energy, he had plunged into the wonderful literature of the subject, and as, without the prejudice which had formerly darkened his brain, he read the illuminating testimony of Hare, de Morgan, Crookes, Lombroso, Barrett, Lodge, and so many other great men, he marvelled that he could ever for one instant have imagined that such a consensus of opinion could be founded upon error. His violent and wholehearted nature made him take up the psychic cause with the same vehemence, and even occasionally the same intolerance with which he had once denounced it, and the old lion bared his teeth and roared back at those who had once been his associates.

His remarkable article in the *Spectator* began, "The obtuse incredulity and stubborn unreason of the prelates who refused to look through the telescope of Galileo and to observe the moons of Jupiter, has been far transcended in our own days by those noisy controversialists, who rashly express extreme opinions upon those psychic matters which they have never had either the time, or the inclination to examine"; while in a final sentence he expressed his conviction that his opponents "did not in truth represent the thought of the twentieth century, but might rather be regarded as mental fossils dug from some early Pliocene horizon." Critics raised their hands in horror, as is their wont, against the robust language of the article, though violence of attack has for so many years been condoned in the case of those who are in opposition. So we may leave Challenger, his black mane slowly turning to grey, but his great brain growing ever stronger and more virile as it faces such problems as the future had in store—a future which had ceased to be bounded by the narrow horizon of death, and which now stretches away into the infinite possibilities and developments of continued survival of personality, character and work. . . .

[The story ends with the marriage of the narrator and Challenger's daughter. After listing the living guests, the narrator speculates on the possible presence of spirit guests.]

All these and many more were visible to our two-inch spectrum of colour, and audible to our four octaves of sound. How many others, outside those narrow limitations, may have added their presence and their blessing —who shall say?

For Conan Doyle, however, the real proof was not other people's observations but his own. "All fine-drawn theories of the subconscious go to pieces before the plain statement of the intelligence, 'I am a spirit. I am Innes. I am your brother,'" he asserted. He believed in the claims of spiritualism because he had seen spirits, heard them, and touched them. "I have seen my mother and my nephew . . . as plainly as ever I saw them in life," he wrote. "I have smelt the peculiar ozone-like smell of ectoplasm.... I have seen spirits walk round the room in fair light and join in the talk of the company. . . . If a man could see, hear, and feel all this, and yet remain unconvinced of unseen intelligent forces around him, he would have good cause to doubt his own sanity." One of Conan Doyle's last works, published in 1926, shows how an intelligent, skeptical, and scientific man can be converted to spiritualism. *The Land of Mist* brings back Professor Challenger, the discoverer of dinosaurs, to challenge the spiritualists, only to discover by objective experience that they are correct.

Conan Doyle saw his own conversion to spiritualism as scientifically rational in the same way. "I trust that the record of my previous life will assure the reader that I have within my limitations preserved a sane and balanced judgment, since I have never hitherto been extreme in my views, and since what I have said has so often been endorsed by the actual course of events," he writes at the end of *Memories and Adventures*. He did not deny the presence of fakes and frauds among the spiritualists. He called such deception, "the most odious and blasphemous crime which a human being can commit." But he was confident of his ability to detect trickery if it was present.

However, he was more gullible than he believed. Writing in the thirties, Harry Price, a specialist in debunking spiritualist frauds, explained, "Too honest himself, he could not imagine his sympathetic credulity being imposed upon." He was completely taken in by some hoaxes of the time. One egregious episode was his support of the so-called Cottingley fairies. Immediately after the war, two little girls in the village of Cottingley in northern England (who years later admitted they had been faking) claimed that they had captured on film images of fairies from the stream behind their house. Their photographs came to Conan Doyle's attention, and he became one of their most ardent supporters, first in a long article in *The Strand Magazine*, and then in his book *The Coming of the Fairies*. Seeing the fairies as a different kind of proof of the existence of a spiritual world, he wrote, "It is no exaggeration to say that they will mark an epoch in human thought. The recognition of their existence will jolt the material twentieth century out of its heavy ruts in the mud, and will make it admit that there is a glamour and mystery to life." Conan Doyle also came out in favor of such legends as the "Mummy's Curse," which, it was claimed, killed off members of the expeditions that broke open the tombs of the pharaohs of Egypt.

The great magician and escape artist Harry Houdini, who became a friend of Conan Doyle's in 1920, thought Conan Doyle was being taken in by magic tricks. "He is good-natured, very bright, but a monomaniac on the subject of Spiritualism," Houdini wrote. "Being uninitiated in the world of mystery, never having been taught the artifices of conjuring, it was the simplest thing in the world for anyone to gain his confidence and hoodwink him." Conan Doyle believed that Houdini actually had supernatural powers without realizing it, and was unconvinced by Houdini's denials. Conan Doyle's wife Jean had developed the power of channeling spirit writings, and she received a message from Houdini's dead mother, which she passed on to him. Houdini rejected it, pointing out that his Jewish mother would not have begun her message with the sign of the cross, and would not have written in English, because she had spoken only Yiddish. Conan Doyle could not forgive this doubt of his wife, and brought an end to the friendship.

Once he was convinced of the validity of spiritualism, its physical proofs were not very important to Conan Doyle, and he grew impatient with newspapers that concentrated only on debating the validity of seances, spirit writing, and such phenomena. "Of course, these physical phenomena have a use of their own," he has a spiritualist explain in *The Land of Mist*. "They rivet the attention of the inquirer and encourage him to go further. Personally, hav-

A poster advertising a New Jersey appearance of magician and escape artist Harry Houdini. Eventually the conflict between Houdini's determination to disprove the claims of spiritualism and Conan Doyle's determination to believe them destroyed the friendship between the two men.

ing seen them all, I would not go across the road to see them again. But I would go across many roads to get high messages from the beyond."

The truly important feature for Conan Doyle was that spiritualism finally provided him with the moral and religious framework he had been seeking all his life, while avoiding the intolerance and narrow-mindedness that had turned him away from conventional religions so many years before. By the light of spiritualism, all religions were partial but valid expressions of the same truth, and there was no need to consign all members outside one sect to damnation. In *If I Could Preach Just Once,* he wrote, "There is nothing which makes the monstrous claim that God supports one clique of mankind against another. . . . If a man be kindly and gentle, there is no fear for him in the beyond whether he is or is not the member of any recognized Church on earth." Or as one of the spirit visitors in *The Land of Mist* says simply, "All religions are right if they make you better."

Conan Doyle threw himself into the cause of spiritualism with the enthusiasm and selfless energy he always devoted to what he believed was important. In the remaining 15 years of his life, he published 13 books on spiritualism, as well as many articles. He ceased almost completely to write on other subjects, although he could have named his own price for any fiction he cared to turn out. To the editor of *The Strand,* who asked him for a story, he replied, "I wish I could do as you wish, but, as you know, my life is devoted to one end and at present I can't see any literature which would be of any use to you above the horizon. I can only write what comes to me." He believed that his popularity as a fiction writer had been given to him so that people would listen to his spiritualist message. After recruiting Professor Challenger to the cause in *The Land of Mist,* he wrote to the editor of *The Strand,* "Thank God that book is done! It was so important that I feared I might pass away before it was finished."

Whenever possible, Conan Doyle took his entire family with him on his extensive trips to spread the gospel of spiritualism. The family posed during a visit to Hollywood in 1923. From left to right are Denis, Conan Doyle's wife Jean, his daughter Jean, Conan Doyle, Adrian, and June Mathis of Goldwyn Studios.

Given this attitude, it is perhaps surprising that he never tried to use his most famous creation, Sherlock Holmes, to promote spiritualism. The Holmes of the later stories is much more philosophical and inclined to speculate on the meaning of life, but, although the stories continued to appear almost through the end of Conan Doyle's life, Holmes never expresses any belief in a spiritual world. In fact, in one of the last stories, published in 1924, "The Adventure of the Sussex Vampire," he says to Watson, "Are we to give serious attention to such things? This agency stands flat-footed upon the ground, and there it must remain. The world is big enough for us. No ghosts need apply." Perhaps the artist in Conan Doyle convinced him that there was no way Sherlock Holmes could plausibly be made into a spiritualist. Or perhaps he was showing his true opinion of his less-than-favorite character. He may have thought Holmes was the kind of person he describes in his autobiography as, "a class of investigator who . . . trips continually over his own brains. . . . His intellect becomes a positive curse to him, for he uses it to avoid the straight road and to fashion out some strange devious path."

Conan Doyle lectured on spiritualism throughout Great Britain, Australia, and South Africa, and attempted to speak in the capitals of every country in Europe. He made two separate trips to the United States, during which he covered 55,000 miles and addressed a quarter of a million people. He devoted his modest fortune to the cause, spending vast sums on his lecture tours, and founding his own psychic bookstore, press, and museum, run by his daughter Mary Louise. In 1926, he published his history of spiritualism at his own expense.

He was willing to risk sacrificing even the remarkable affection the public felt toward him to the cause. He knew the kind of scorn he could expect on the subject of the spiritualists—he puts a good deal of it into Professor Challenger's mouth at the beginning of *The Land of Mist*. "There seems to me to be absolutely no limit to the inanity and credulity of the human race," Challenger exclaims. "Homo Sapiens! Homo Idioticus! Who do they pray to— the ghosts?" But the chivalrous knight would not be deterred from his quest by a fear of ridicule. Actually, the public treated Conan Doyle with surprising tolerance. His spiritualist lectures were well attended and kindly received, although probably few of the people who came to hear him because he was Sir Arthur Conan Doyle were actually converted. Critics spoke disparagingly of his beliefs, but most continued to honor his sincerity and personal integrity even as they claimed he had been duped.

In the United States, his unusual courtesy to the press on his previous visits was now rewarded. The American newspapers, which usually tended to seize any chance to poke fun at prominent figures, confined themselves to basic reporting on the subject of his talks and the crowd that attended. He did encounter some abuse, of course, such as the Catholic convert who wrote to him that he should be horsewhipped, but he did not let such comments concern him. "This controversy with bumptious and ignorant people is a mere passing thing which matters nothing," he remarked.

Finally, Conan Doyle sacrificed his life to spiritualism. Despite his prodigious strength and vigor, he had begun suffering heart trouble during the war, and his doctors warned him that if he worked too hard he would kill himself. He paid no attention to their warnings, feeling that the work was too important. In 1929, he insisted on delivering an Armistice Day speech in London's Albert Hall and then in Queen's Hall—and then repeating it outside in the snow for the overflow crowd. He collapsed and was ill for several months. He seemed to be recovering, but on July 7, 1930, he suffered a heart attack and died. He was conscious until death, sitting in his chair surrounded by his family, and he was unafraid. The year of his death, he had revised his autobiography, ending it with the statement, "The reader will

Conan Doyle drew this cartoon summary of the various aspects of his eventful life late in 1929. It reflects his own evaluation of their importance, and thus spiritualism looms larger than Sherlock Holmes. He states optimistically that with a little rest the old horse would soon be "back on the road once more"; however, he was dead within a year.

judge that I have had many adventures. The greatest and most glorious of all awaits me now."

His epitaph commemorates him as the chivalrous knight: STEEL STRAIGHT, BLADE TRUE. ARTHUR CONAN DOYLE. KNIGHT, PATRIOT, PHYSICIAN & MAN OF LETTERS. Perhaps equally apt, if less lofty, as a summary of his life is this tribute from the master of a trawler he once sailed on: "You can fight, mend a broken leg or any other wound and write a true account of it all when it is all over."

Modern versions of Sherlock Holmes appear in all sorts of unexpected places. This is Sherlock Hemlock,
"the world's greatest detective," a Muppet from the PBS children's television show Sesame Street.

Epilogue

If Conan Doyle's spirit is still around, as he believed it would be, he must be surprised and disappointed at the way he is remembered today. Although the spiritualist church still survives, the fierce devotion that Conan Doyle gave to it is almost forgotten. His spiritualist books are rarely read. His literary works have fared somewhat better—the stories about Brigadier Gerard and Professor Challenger and the novel *The White Company* are still in print and can be found in libraries—but Conan Doyle's reputation does not rest on them. Only Sherlock Holmes, whose value Conan Doyle never fully understood, still survives with the same popularity he had when his author was alive.

Sherlock Holmes has taken on a life beyond the stories written by Conan Doyle. Many other writers have produced Sherlock Holmes stories, most notably Nicholas Meyer, beginning with *The Seven-Per-Cent Solution*. More movies have been made about Holmes than any other character, real or historical. Both William Baring-Gould and Vincent Starrett have even written biographies of Holmes. The Abbey National Building Society, which today occupies 221B Baker Street, employs a staff member whose job is to act as Holmes's secretary, answering the approximately 50 letters he still receives each week.

In the modern world, Arthur Conan Doyle's creation threatens to obscure his creator. Sherlock Holmes's greatest fans come close to denying Conan Doyle's existence. The many Sherlock Holmes clubs around the world, of which the oldest and most celebrated is the New York Baker Street Irregulars, predicate their activities on the claim that Conan Doyle did not invent Holmes or his adventures—they were real. Starting from this premise, they foster scholarship that examines seeming contradictions and impossibilities in the stories (of which there are many, because Conan Doyle was concerned only with telling a good story and made no attempt to be accurate or consistent) and explains how these circumstances "really happened." Fans refer to this activity as "the higher criticism." According to the text (known as the "Canon"), John Watson, not Conan Doyle, wrote the stories. So what role is left for Conan Doyle? To the Baker Street Irregulars he is only "the Agent"; his name is not mentioned.

Almost from his very first published story, Conan Doyle created characters and events so convincing that his readers thought they were real. With his immortal character Sherlock Holmes, he has accomplished perhaps the ultimate success for a writer of fiction—the creation is so real that he has taken on his own life and broken free of his creator.

CHRONOLOGY

1859
Arthur Conan Doyle born on May 22 in Edinburgh, Scotland

1869–74
Attends Stonyhurst, a school run by Jesuits

1875
Studies at Feldkirch School in Austria

1879–81
Works toward a medical degree at Edinburgh University

1879
Publishes first story, "The Mystery of Sasassa Valley"

1880
Serves as ship's surgeon on the *Hope* during an Arctic voyage

1881
Becomes a Bachelor of Medicine and Master of Surgery

1881–82
Serves as ship's doctor on the *Mayumba,* which travels along the west coast of Africa

1882
Moves to Southsea in Portsmouth in July after a brief partnership with Dr. George Budd, and attempts to set up a private medical practice

1885
Marries Louise "Touie" Hawkins on August 6

1887
Publishes *A Study in Scarlet,* first appearance of Sherlock Holmes, in *Beeton's Christmas Annual*

1889
First child, Mary Louise, is born; *Micah Clarke,* first major novel, is published

1890

Publishes second Sherlock Holmes novel, *The Sign of Four,* and the historical novel *The White Company*; leaves Portsmouth for Vienna to study ophthalmology

1891

Attempts, unsuccessfully, to establish himself as an eye specialist in London. Starting in July, the first six Sherlock Holmes short stories are published in *The Strand Magazine* and create a sensation

1892

18 more Sherlock Holmes stories appear; first son, Alleyne Kingsley, is born

1893

In the December issue of *The Strand Magazine,* Sherlock Holmes dies in "The Final Problem"; Conan Doyle's father dies; Touie is diagnosed with tuberculosis, and Conan Doyle moves with her to Davos, Switzerland, for her health

1894

Goes on a lecture tour of the United States

1895

Visits Egypt and travels to the front during the Sudan War hoping to witness battle firsthand

1896

Returns to England

1897

Settles into the mansion, "Undershaw," he has built in Surrey; on March 15, meets and falls in love with Jean Leckie

1900

Serves for seven months during the Boer War as head of a field hospital in South Africa; writes *The Great Boer War;* runs for a seat in Parliament, representing the Unionist Party, but loses the election

1901

Brings back Sherlock Holmes in *The Hound of the Baskervilles*

1902

Knighted for his book in which he defends British conduct in the Boer War

1903

Resurrects Sherlock Holmes in "The Adventure of the Empty House" in the October issue of *The Strand*

1906

Touie dies in July; Conan Doyle fights for justice in the case of George Edalji; he stands for Parliament again, but is defeated

1907

Marries Jean Leckie

1909

Second son, Denis Percy Stewart, is born; Conan Doyle is approached by Roger Morel to help press for reform in the Belgian Congo

1910

Begins his attempt to obtain justice in the case of Oscar Slater; third son, Adrian Malcolm, is born

1911

Participates in the International Road Competition

1912

Publishes *The Lost World,* the first appearance of Professor Challenger; second daughter, Lena Jean, is born

1914

Travels to the Canadian west; publishes final Sherlock Holmes novel, *The Valley of Fear;* when World War I is declared, attempts, unsuccessfully, to enlist, then establishes a Civilian Reserve Corps

1915

Converts to spiritualism, probably after receiving a message from beyond the grave

1918

Oldest son, Alleyne Kingsley, dies in the influenza epidemic after being weakened by war wounds

1919

Brother Innes dies of pneumonia; Conan Doyle begins the crusade on behalf of spiritualism which will occupy the rest of his life

1927

The final Sherlock Holmes story, "The Adventure of Shoscombe Old Place," appears; largely as a result of Conan Doyle's work on his behalf, Oscar Slater is finally released from prison

1930

Conan Doyle suffers a heart attack and dies on July 7

FURTHER READING

The best source for information on Arthur Conan Doyle is his own autobiography, *Memories and Adventures.* All his letters and papers have been tied up in lawsuits and unavailable since the early 1930s, shortly after his death. Only John Lamond, John Dickson Carr, and Pierre Nordon were able to see these papers before they were withdrawn. Every biography that has been published since that time has been restricted to the material they quoted.

WORKS ABOUT ARTHUR CONAN DOYLE AND SHERLOCK HOLMES

Baring-Gould, William Stuart. *Sherlock Holmes of Baker Street: The Life of the World's First Consulting Detective.* New York: Random House, 1995. A "biography" of the great detective.

Carr, John Dickson. *The Life of Sir Arthur Conan Doyle.* London: John Murray; New York: Harper, 1949. Carr, a mystery writer, collaborated with Adrian Conan Doyle on several Sherlock Holmes adventures. His entertaining biography reads like a novel and is not strictly factual.

Cooke, Ivan, ed. *The Return of Arthur Conan Doyle.* Liss, Hampshire, England: White Eagle Publishing Trust, 1980. Part two of this book, "The Message of Arthur Conan Doyle," was supposedly written by Arthur Conan Doyle after his death, through the medium Grace Cooke.

Costello, Peter. *The Real World of Sherlock Holmes: The True Crimes Investigated by Arthur Conan Doyle.* New York: Carroll & Graf, 1991.

Doyle, Adrian Conan. *The True Conan Doyle.* New York: Coward-McCann, 1946. Adrian Conan Doyle wrote this pamphlet to refute Hesketh Pearson's biography of his father, in which, he believed, Pearson had belittled Arthur Conan Doyle.

Edwards, Owen Dudley. *The Quest for Sherlock Holmes: A Biographical Study of Arthur Conan Doyle.* Totowa, N.J.: Barnes & Noble, 1983.

Hall, Trevor H., with contributions by Charles O. Ellison. *Sherlock Holmes and His Creator.* London: Duckworth, 1978.

Higham, Charles. *The Adventures of Conan Doyle: The Life of the*

Creator of Sherlock Holmes. New York: Norton, 1976.

Jaffe, Jacqueline A. *Arthur Conan Doyle.* Boston: Twayne, 1987.

Lachtman, Howard. *Sherlock Slept Here: Being a Brief History of the Singular Adventures of Sir Arthur Conan Doyle in America, with Some Observations upon the Exploits of Mr. Sherlock Holmes.* Santa Barbara, Calif.: Capra, 1985.

Lamond, John. *Arthur Conan Doyle, A Memoir, by the Rev. John Lamond, D. D., with an Epilogue by Lady Conan Doyle.* 1931. Reprint, Port Washington, N.Y.: Kennikat, 1972. This authorized biography, written with the help of Conan Doyle's second wife, concentrates on spiritualism.

Lellenberg, Jon L., with a foreword by Jean Conan Doyle. *The Quest for Sir Arthur Conan Doyle: Thirteen Biographers in Search of a Life.* Carbondale: Southern Illinois University Press, 1987. A study of all the available biographies of Conan Doyle.

"The Man Who Believed in Fairies," *Smithsonian Magazine,* September 1997, p. 6. The story of Arthur Conan Doyle and the Cottingley fairies.

Nordon, Pierre. *Conan Doyle: A Biography.* Translated by Frances Partridge. New York: Holt, Rinehart and Winston, 1967. An extremely thorough and scholarly biography, probably the most complete biography available.

Pearson, Hesketh. *Conan Doyle, His Life and Art.* London: Methuen, 1943; New York: Walker, 1961. Pearson's portrait of Conan Doyle as a shallow and ordinary man inspired Adrian Conan Doyle to write a rebuttal.

Rodin, Alvin E., and Jack D. Key. *The Medical Casebook of Doctor Arthur Conan Doyle: From Practitioner to Sherlock Holmes and Beyond.* Malabar, Fla.: R. E. Krieger, 1984.

Stashower, Daniel. *Teller of Tales: The Life of Arthur Conan Doyle.* New York: Henry Holt, 1999. The most recent biography of Arthur Conan Doyle.

Starrett, Vincent. *The Private Life of Sherlock Holmes.* 1933. Reprint, New York: Haskell House, 1971.

Stavert, Geoffrey. *A Study in Southsea: The Unrevealed Life of Doctor Arthur Conan Doyle.* Horndean, Portsmouth, Hampshire: Milestone, 1987. This study contains everything that can be known about Conan Doyle's first few years on his own.

WORKS BY ARTHUR CONAN DOYLE

AUTOBIOGRAPHICAL:

Doyle, Arthur Conan. *Letters to the Press.* Edited by John M. Gibson and Richard L. Green. Iowa City: University of Iowa Press, 1986.

——. *Memories and Adventures.* Boston: Little, Brown, 1924.

——. *Pheneas Speaks: Direct Spirit Communications in the Family Circle.* London: The Psychic Press and Bookshop, 1927. The story of the Conan Doyles' seances.

Orel, Harold, ed. *Sir Arthur Conan Doyle: Interviews and Recollections.* New York: St. Martin's, 1991.

SHERLOCK HOLMES

Doyle, Arthur Conan. *The Adventures of Sherlock Holmes.* Edited with an introduction by Richard Lancelyn Green. New York: Oxford University Press, 1993.

——. *The Annotated Sherlock Holmes: The Four Novels and the Fifty-Six Short Stories Complete.* Edited with an introduction, notes, and bibliography by William S. Baring-Gould. New York: C. N. Potter, 1967.

——. *The Case-Book of Sherlock Holmes.* Edited with an introduction by W. W. Robson. New York: Oxford University Press, 1993.

——. *The Hound of the Baskervilles.* Edited with an introduction by W. W. Robson. New York: Oxford University Press, 1993.

——. *His Last Bow.* Edited with an introduction by Owen Dudley Edwards. New York: Oxford University Press, 1993.

——. *The Memoirs of Sherlock Holmes.* Edited with an introduction by Christopher Roden. New York: Oxford University Press, 1993.

——. *The Return of Sherlock Holmes.* Edited with an introduction by Richard Lancelyn Green. New York: Oxford University Press, 1993.

——. *The Sign of the Four.* Edited with an introduction by Christopher Roden. New York: Oxford University Press, 1994.

——. *A Study in Scarlet.* Edited with an introduction by Owen Dudley Edwards. New York: Oxford University Press, 1993.

——. *The Valley of Fear.* Edited with an introduction by Owen Dudley Edwards. New York: Oxford University Press, 1993.

OTHER WORKS

Doyle, Arthur Conan. *The Best Science Fiction of Arthur Conan Doyle.* Edited by Charles G. Waugh and Martin H. Greenberg, with an introduction by George E. Slusser. Carbondale: Southern Illinois University Press, 1981.

——. *The Best Supernatural Tales of Arthur Conan Doyle.* Selected and introduced by E. F. Bleiler. New York: Dover, 1979.

——. *The Exploits of Brigadier Gerard.* Edited and introduced by Owen Dudley Edwards. Edinburgh: Canongate, 1991.

——. *The Land of Mist.* London: Hutchinson, 1926.

——. *The Lost World: Being an Account of the Recent Amazing Adventures of Professor George E. Challenger, Lord John Roxton, Professor Summerlee, and Mr. E. D. Malone of the Daily Gazette.* Introduced by Ian Duncan. New York: Oxford University Press, 1995.

——. *Micah Clarke: His Statement As Made to His Three Grandchildren, Joseph, Gervas, & Reuben, During the Hard Winter of 1734.* 1889. Reprint, New York: Harper, 1929.

——. *The Professor Challenger Adventures: The Lost World and The Poison Belt.* San Francisco: Chronicle, 1989.

——. *The Stark Munro Letters: Being a Series of Sixteen Letters Written by J. Stark Munro, M.B., to His Friend and Former Fellow-Student, Herbert Swanborough, of Lowell, Massachusetts, during the Years 1881–1884. Edited and Arranged by A. Conan Doyle.* 1895. Reprint, Bloomington, Ind.: Gaslight, 1982.

——. *The White Company.* Illustrated by N. C. Wyeth. New York: Morrow Junior Books, 1988.

INDEX

ACKNOWLEDGMENTS

I would like to thank:

Harriet Sigerman, without whom this book would never have happened.

Naomi B. Pascal and Deborah Brodie, for piercing editorial insights, gently expressed.

Paul Pascal, for his guidance and impressive erudition.

David and Susan Pascal for helpful feedback and support.

Nancy Toff and Lisa Barnett at Oxford University Press, for their assistance and (especially) patience.

David Lupher, for his research prowess.

PICTURE CREDITS

Martin Booth: 2, 10, 36, 55, 56, 94; © 1999 Children's Television Workshop. © 1999 Jim Henson Company: 144; William Andrews Clark Memorial Library, University of California, Los Angeles: 66; Corbis-Bettman: 6, 138, 140; Paul Costello: 87; Richard Lancelyn Green: 28, 29, 33, 46, 47, 48, 61, 63, 76, 82, 83, 88, 98, 103, 116, 120, 130; Robert Krieger Publishing: 23, 142; University of Minnesota, Sherlock Holmes Collection: 40, 68, 92; General Research Division, The New York Public Library, Astor, Lenox and Tilden Foundations: 73; Photofest: 104, 105, 122; Robinson Publishing: 110, 113; Royal College of Surgeons of Edinburgh: 20, 21, 25.

TEXT CREDITS

pp. 28–29: Doyle, Arthur Conan. *A Study in Scarlet*. Edited with an introduction by Owen Dudley Edwards. New York: Oxford University Press, 1993.

pp. 41–42: Doyle, Arthur Conan. *The Stark Munro Letters: Being a Series of Sixteen Letters Written by J. Stark Munro, M.B., to His Friend and Former Fellow-Student, Herbert Swanborough, of Lowell, Massachusetts, during the Years 1881–1884. Edited and Arranged by A. Conan Doyle*. 1895. Reprint, Bloomington, Ind.: Gaslight, 1982.

pp. 80–81: Doyle, Arthur Conan. *The Memoirs of Sherlock Holmes*. Edited with an introduction by Christopher Roden. New York: Oxford University Press, 1993.

p. 101: Doyle, Arthur Conan. *His Last Bow*. Edited with an introduction by Owen Dudley Edwards. New York: Oxford University Press, 1993.

p. 124: Doyle, Arthur Conan. *The Lost World: Being an Account of the Recent Amazing Adventures of Professor George E. Challenger, Lord John Roxton, Professor Summerlee, and Mr. E. D. Malone of the Daily Gazette*. Introduced by Ian Duncan. New York: Oxford University Press, 1995.

pp. 134–35: Doyle, Arthur Conan. *The Land of Mist*. London: Hutchinson, 1926.

As a child, **Janet B. Pascal** used to play Sherlock Holmes trivia games with her father and brother, and can still tell you whose shoes were stolen from outside the hotel room, and what kind of tires the solitary cyclist used. She studied English history and literature at Harvard and Yale, and now works for a major children's publishing house. This is her first book. Originally from Seattle, she now lives in New York City.